Cambridge English

Business
BENCHMARK

Upper Intermediate
BULATS and Business Vantage

T0343092

Personal Study Book

Guy Brook-Hart

CAMBRIDGE
UNIVERSITY PRESS

University Printing House, Cambridge CB2 8BS, United Kingdom

One Liberty Plaza, 20th Floor, New York, NY 10006, USA

477 Williamstown Road, Port Melbourne, VIC 3207, Australia

314–321, 3rd Floor, Plot 3, Splendor Forum, Jasola District Centre,
New Delhi – 110025, India

79 Anson Road, #06–04/06, Singapore 079906

Cambridge University Press is part of the University of Cambridge.

It furthers the University's mission by disseminating knowledge in the pursuit of
education, learning and research at the highest international levels of excellence.

www.cambridge.org
Information on this title: www.cambridge.org/9781107686601

© Cambridge University Press 2013

First published 2006
Second edition published 2013
Reprinted 2019

Printed in Great Britain by CPI Group (UK) Ltd, Croydon CR0 4YY

A catalogue record for this publication is available from the British Library

ISBN 978-1-107-68660-1 Upper Intermediate BULATS and Business Vantage
Personal Study Book
ISBN 978-1-107-63211-0 Upper Intermediate BULATS and Business Vantage
Teacher's Resource Book
ISBN 978-1-107-68098-2 Upper Intermediate Business Vantage Student's Book
ISBN 978-1-107-63983-6 Upper Intermediate BULATS Student's Book
ISBN 978-1-107-68003-6 Upper Intermediate BULATS Class Audio CDs (2)
ISBN 978-1-107-63315-5 Upper Intermediate Business Vantage Class Audio CDs (2)

Author's note

To the student

This Personal Study Book provides you with two pages of extra exercises and activities for each unit of the Student's Book. The exercises and activities are designed to reinforce what you have studied and they cover vocabulary, grammar, reading and writing.

It is a good idea to do the work in each unit of the Personal Study Book after you have finished the corresponding unit in the Student's Book. This will help you to remember things you have studied. You will need to write your answers in your notebook. Do the exercises regularly while the things you have studied in the Student's Book are still fresh in your memory.

Check your answers by looking in the key on pages 69–80. If you are not sure why an answer in the key is correct, ask your teacher to explain.

When you do the writing exercises, you can compare your answer with a sample answer in the key. If your teacher agrees, you can give him/her your answer to correct.

If you are preparing for the *Cambridge English: Business Vantage* exam or the BULATS test, many of the exercises are designed to give you exam practice.

The Personal Study Book also contains a 15-page Writing supplement, which covers a number of areas that students at your level often have difficulty with. These are: punctuation and spelling; writing in paragraphs; and generally organising your writing in a clear and logical manner. Take time to work through the Writing supplement methodically, doing all the tasks. Don't leave it till the end of your course. When you're not sure about what you have written, hand your writing in to your teacher and ask him/her to correct it and comment on it with you. The sooner you start work on it and the more you write, the sooner your writing will improve, giving you greater satisfaction and leading to higher grades in homework and exams.

Acknowledgements

The author and publishers acknowledge the following sources of copyright material and are grateful for the permissions granted. While every effort has been made, it has not always been possible to identify the sources of all the material used, or to trace all copyright holders. If any omissions are brought to our notice, we will be happy to include the appropriate acknowledgements on reprinting.

Petpals (UK) Limited for the text on p.24 adapted from 'Why Brendan is Animal Crackers', www.petpals.com. Reproduced with permission; Time Inc for the text on p.38 adapted from 'What the Web Taught FedEX' by Owen Thomas, *Business 2.0 Magazine*, 18/11/04. Copyright © 2004 Time Inc. Used under licence.

Front cover photography by: Shutterstock/Serp
Illustrations by: Simon Tegg
Design and layout: Hart McLeod Ltd.
Project manager: Jane Coates

Editor: Catriona Watson-Brown
Production controller: Liz Knowelden
Managing editor: Una Yeung
Publisher: Karen Barns

Contents

Staff development and training

Vocabulary

Complete the text below with the words and phrases in the box.

certificates   degree   development   employees   experience   qualifications   ~~recruit~~
skills   training   training course

Our company uses a professional agency to **1** _recruit_ new **2** .... The
company is a management consultancy, so most new workers have a university
3 .... , even if they are too young to have very much work **4** .... The
company really believes in staff **5** .... All new employees are given a two-week
6 .... , when they start to learn about the company and its working methods.
This is followed by further on-the-job **7** .... so that they can learn the necessary
8 .... to do their work well. They also need the professional
9 .... which are expected by our clients – **10** .... and diplomas and so on.

Grammar

1 Are these words countable (C) or uncountable (U)? Where necessary,
  use a dictionary to help you.

1 advice _U_	**18** machine
2 cargo	**19** postal mail
3 comment	**20** page
4 computer program	**21** printing paper
5 cost	**22** price
6 email	**23** recruitment
7 equipment	**24** research
8 fact	**25** software
9 feedback	**26** spending
10 freight	**27** study
11 holiday	**28** team
12 information	**29** teamwork
13 job	**30** training
14 journey	**31** training course
15 knowledge	**32** transport
16 sick leave (time off work)	**33** travel
17 lorry	**34** work

2 Complete this job advertisement with *a/an* if the noun is countable and singular. Leave the gap blank if the noun is uncountable or plural.

Looking for 1 .....−..... work in 2 .....an..... advertising agency? Publicity Plus is recruiting 3 .... trainee writer to work with the creative team on 4 .... advertisements in a range of sectors. You may also from time to time be asked to write 5 .... advertisement or leaflet. 6 .... formal qualifications are not necessary, but 7 .... experience in 8 .... marketing is desirable. We are offering 9 .... permanent contract to the right person. 10 .... satisfactory performance will lead to 11 .... quick promotion. For the right person, our company is 12 .... business with 13 .... future! For more 14 .... information, write to info@publicityplus.com.

3 Complete the questions below with the question words or phrases in the box. You will not need all the words/phrases.

how   how long   how many   how much   how often   what   when   where
which   ~~who~~   why

1   ....Who.... is your boss? Ms Jones?

2   .... have you worked for this company?

3   .... office would you prefer to work in: company headquarters or a regional office?

4   .... did you go to school – in this country or abroad?

5   .... do you go on holiday – once a year or more often?

6   .... job would you like to be doing in ten years' time?

7   .... people work in your office?

8   .... would you like to earn?

4 Put the words into the correct order to form questions.

1   enjoy / job / do / about / What / your / most / you / ?
    What do you enjoy most about your job?

2   your / there / about / you / job / anything / Is / dislike / ?

3   How / travel / you / to / often / job / for / have / do / your / ?

4   many / are / your / employees / there / How / company / in / ?

5   work / of / line / this / into / get / you / did / How / ?

6   What / think / years' / you / time / you / in / will / be / do / doing / ten / ?

2 Job descriptions and job satisfaction

Vocabulary

1 Complete the text below with the words and phrases in the box.

> budget   deadlines   launch   projects   results   targets   team leaders   ~~teams~~

> In my company, nearly all work is done in 1 ...*teams*.. , so all our managers are
> 2 .... I found this quite easy to adapt to, because at Business School we
> worked together a lot on 3 .... , and this got me used to working towards
> goals or 4 .... and meeting 5 ....
> I work in Research and Development, and we get real satisfaction from taking
> new products through from the original idea to the 6 .... perhaps one or two
> years later. I'm a financial manager, so a lot of my work involves ensuring that we
> get the best possible 7 .... from our projects while keeping within 8 ....
> limits – and that involves strict cost control.

2 Complete this table with the missing word forms.

verb	noun	adjective
1 *satisfy*	satisfaction	2
develop	3	4
supervise	5	6
manage	7	8
recruit	9	
10	11	challenging
	12	responsible
perform	13	
invest	14	
15	finance	16
promote	17	18
effect	19	20

Grammar

1 a Complete the text below with a verb from the box in the correct tense – past simple or present perfect.

> be become do encourage ~~joined~~ move pass spend work

> I **1** *joined* BP as a graduate trainee four years ago. I **2** .... just three months in the production department and then they **3** .... me to marketing. Since then, I **4** .... in three different divisions of the company and I **5** .... an overseas posting as well – I **6** .... Assistant Divisional Manager in Venezuela for six months last year. The company **7** .... me to continue training, and last month I **8** .... my professional exams and **9** .... a member of the Institute of Chartered Engineers.

b Write a similar paragraph to describe your own student or professional career.

2 Study this chart, which shows staff numbers in an Austrian engineering company, and complete the extract below from the report by putting the verbs in brackets into the correct tenses.

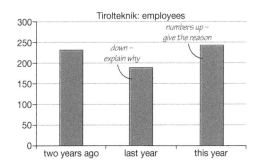

Tirolteknik: employees

numbers up – give the reason
down – explain why

> Two years ago, Tirolteknik **1** *employed* (employ) 230 members of staff, most of whom **2** .... (work) on large-scale state-funded projects in western Austria. However, last year the government **3** .... (decide) to reduce its budget, so the company **4** .... (have) to temporarily lay off 40 employees. Fortunately, this year the company **5** .... (sign) contracts to equip two large factories in the region, with the result that it **6** .... (be) necessary to take on 50 extra staff.

3 Write a paragraph for a report on this Russian company using the handwritten notes. Use the paragraph from Exercise 2 as a model.

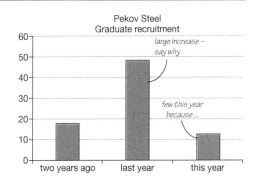

Pekov Steel
Graduate recruitment

large increase – say why
few this year because ...

Grammar

Complete this email of enquiry by putting the correct preposition in each gap.

Dear Sir or Madam,

I am a 22-year-old student **1** ....*of*.... psychology **2** .... the University of Hanover in Germany and I am writing to enquire **3** .... career opportunities **4** .... your company. I have visited your website and I see that you have an innovative and open-minded approach **5** .... the recruitment and management **6** .... personnel within your company. I am **7** .... my final year of a five-year course of studies and am particularly interested **8** .... working **9** .... the area of personnel recruitment. My particular specialisation is psychometric testing, and **10** .... my final project, I have investigated the efficiency of such tests **11** .... predicting the work performance of prospective employees. I would be most grateful if you could send me information **12** .... what opportunities exist in your company, either **13** .... a graduate trainee **14** .... a year's time or for an internship **15** .... the near future. Could you also tell me how I should apply?

Thanking you **16** .... advance.

Yours faithfully,

Reading

Read this email of application. In most lines, there is one extra word. It is either grammatically incorrect or does not fit in with the meaning of the text. Some lines, however, are correct. If a line is correct, put a tick (✓). If there is an extra word in the line, cross it out.

Dear Sir,	
I am writing ~~for~~ to apply for the post of manager in your new branch	1 *for*
to be opened in Lewisham, as advertised in the *Daily Gazette* of 5 November.	2 ✓
As you will now see from my enclosed curriculum vitae, I am a	3
33-year-old graduate qualification in social sciences from the	4
University of Bristol, with eight years' of experience in management	5
posts within the retail trade, my current position is being that of	6
Assistant Manager at a branch of Dixons in Southampton.	7
Since my leaving university, apart from practical experience in the	8
various posts I have held, although I have studied extensively at	9
night school, attending courses in Negotiating Skills, Personnel	10

Management and Marketing. Dixons have also sent for me on   11
various of internal courses in the same areas.   12
I am so interested in the post advertised because it seems to me   13
to represent the type of opportunity I am looking for – to move into a   14
large international retailing organisation and going to have the   15
experience of setting up a new store from the start.   16
I hope for my application and my curriculum vitae will be of   17
interest to you. I am available for interview at any other time,   18
and my present employers would be happy to supply you a reference.   19
I am look forward to hearing from you.   20
Yours faithfully,

Vocabulary

1 **Complete the sentences below with the words from the box. In some cases, more than one answer is possible.**

> contribute   happy   interested   lucky   ~~passion~~   pride   rewarding   value

1 I have a real *passion* about people and helping them to develop.

2 I take real .... in my company's products and being able to present them to customers.

3 I think what I .... most to my project team is my analytic mindset.

4 I .... the help and support I get from my colleagues in meetings.

5 I'm .... to be working with a global company which offers work opportunities across five continents.

6 I've always been .... in working in IT, right from when I was a small child.

7 It's .... for us to see tangible results for the work we put in.

8 Learning new skills is what really makes me .... – if I go home at the end of the day feeling I've learnt something new, I'm euphoric.

2 **Complete these sentences by forming an adjective from the word in brackets.**

1 I found the training course very *interesting* (*interest*) but a little too long.

2 The report was very .... (*detail*) and highly .... (*inform*).

3 The staff canteen isn't .... (*open*) until ten o'clock.

4 What would be a .... (*convenience*) time for us to meet?

5 I offered her promotion, but she wasn't .... (*interest*).

6 If you are .... (*absence*) from work for more than two days, it's taken out of your annual leave.

4 Making contact

Reading

Complete these two telephone conversations by putting one word in each gap.

Maribel: Finance department. **1** ....*How*.... can I help you?

Manfred: Good morning. Can I speak **2** .... Maribel Arroyo, please?

Maribel: **3** ....

Manfred: Oh, hello. **4** .... is Manfred Steiner from Arts International.

Maribel: Hello, Mr Steiner. What can I do **5** .... you?

Manfred: Well, it's about an invoice – you sent the order we placed, but you forgot to include the invoice, so we can't pay you.

Maribel: Oh, that's not my department, I'm **6** .... , Mr Steiner. That's Mary Slade in Invoicing.

Manfred: OK. Can I speak to her, then, please?

Maribel: Sure. I'll put you **7** ....

Manfred: Thanks very much.

Maribel: Not at **8** ....

Jane: Jane Ashley.

Alan: Oh, hello, Jane, I've been trying to call Tracy, but she's not answering the phone, and it's rather urgent.

Jane: Who is **9** .... , please?

Alan: **10** .... is Alan Searle.

Jane: Oh, hello, Alan, I didn't recognise your voice. I'm **11** .... she's in a meeting at the moment and she's left instructions that she's not to be disturbed. Can I **12** .... a message?

Alan: Yes, can you ask her to call me as soon as **13** .... ?

Jane: Yes, of **14** ....

Alan: **15** .... you very much. Bye.

Jane: Goodbye.

Grammar

1 **Look at the leaflet on the next page from the Skills Development College and complete the report below it by putting the adjectives in brackets into the comparative or superlative form.**

course	Basic Computer Skills	Advanced Computer Skills	Introduction to Accounting
length	4 weeks	6 weeks	10 weeks
hours per week	4	6	8
timetable	Fri. 4–8 p.m.	Mon. and Weds. 9 a.m.–12 p.m.	Mon.–Thurs. 8–10 p.m.
trainees per class	8 max.	6 max.	20 max.
price (per student)	€200	€300	€150

SKILLS DEVELOPMENT COLLEGE

The Skills Development College offers three courses (see accompanying leaflet) which might meet our staff training needs during the next year. The one which is **1** _least useful_ (useful) is the Basic Computer Skills course, since all our staff have basic computer literacy. The Advanced Computer Skills course could be **2** _more appropriate_ (appropriate), especially for some senior managers who have had little time for intensive training. However, it is scheduled at the **3** .... (inconvenient) time on Monday and Wednesday mornings, just when managers are likely to be **4** .... (busy). In addition, the course is **5** .... (expensive), which means that we will be able to give training to **6** .... (few) staff on our present budget. The course which **7** .... (many) of our junior staff could benefit from is the Introduction to Accounting. This is run outside office hours (8–10 p.m. Mon.– Thurs.), which means that it will have **8** .... (little) effect on the running of our offices. However, it is likely to prove **9** .... (costly) than it appears, as we will have to pay overtime to staff attending the course. Also, the **10** .... (large) size of the classes reflects the fact that the course is **11** .... (theoretical) than the computer-skills courses, which have a **12** .... (hands-on) approach.

2 **Each of the sentences in this extract from an in-company training manual contains wrong information for new staff. Correct them by changing the phrases in** *italics* **to the exact opposite. In some cases, more than one answer may be possible.**

Remember, when greeting clients choosing the right words is **1** *much ~~more~~ less important than* the way you dress and your body language. This is because it takes **2** *a little more than* a minute for you to make a first impression and often **3** *much later than* you have had a chance to speak. Once you've made a first impression, it's **4** *much easier* to change it than you think. So, **5** *you needn't prepare* well for that meeting. Dress **6** *slightly less formally than* you normally would in the office. If the meeting is on the phone, remember that your choice of words is **7** *a lot more important than* your tone of voice, so **8** *it really doesn't matter at all* if you sound tired or uninterested.

5 Breaking into the market

Vocabulary

1 Read this text about inventors and choose the best word – A, B, C or D – to fill each gap.

It is not easy for inventors to 1 ...*B*... a new product, especially when they have to 2 .... with large consumer-products companies which have a marketing 3 .... of millions of pounds. Essentially, inventors have to carry out market 4 .... beforehand in order to discover who might need or want their product, and what 5 .... they might be prepared to pay. For a small company, the most effective marketing 6 .... is to demonstrate the product to potential customers first, so that they know what they are buying. 7 .... your marketing efforts on existing customers in order to ensure their 8 .... If you can do that, you will discover that they talk about the product to other people, and 9 .... recommendation is the most cost-effective way of extending your customer base.

Before undertaking costly 10 .... activities, such as printing brochures and taking out advertisements, use your imagination to see if you can reach your 11 .... customers without spending so much. You can 12 .... your product at relatively low cost by handing out free 13 .... at big events, and sending your product to journalists, who, if the product interests them, may write an article about it in a magazine or newspaper. All these activities will raise brand 14 ....

Be ready to sell directly to customers, but, if your product is a consumer product, it is worth approaching retail stores to see if they will 15 .... it, too.

1	A introduce	B launch	C establish	D start
2	A compete	B win	C oppose	D struggle
3	A resource	B fund	C budget	D account
4	A research	B investigations	C tests	D studies
5	A money	B cost	C total	D price
6	A manoeuvre	B scheme	C move	D ploy
7	A Employ	B Focus	C Aim	D Direct
8	A constancy	B presence	C loyalty	D faithfulness
9	A word-of-mouth	B mouth-to-mouth	C face-to-face	D eye-to-eye
10	A publicity	B promotional	C selling	D sales
11	A end	B direct	C target	D objective
12	A communicate	B inform	C announce	D market
13	A examples	B copies	C samples	D pieces
14	A understanding	B awareness	C knowledge	D information
15	A hold	B shelve	C keep	D stock

2 **Find these phrases (1–8) in the Reading text in the Student's Book on page 29, then match them with their definitions (a–h).**

1 take risks
2 word gets around
3 go digital
4 bring in
5 brand ambassador
6 cross over
7 take on
8 fit into

a accept a particular job or responsibility
b ask someone to do a particular job
c do something that might be harmful or dangerous
d lots of people hear about it
e move across to another side
f put on the Internet
g someone who represents the product
h suit

Grammar

Complete this email from the CEO of a company to the Finance Director by putting the verbs in brackets into the correct form: *-ing* form or infinitive.

Dear Colin,

I am writing **1** *to express* (express) my concern about the situation of several of our product lines. Sales appear **2** .... (be) falling in several of them. I suggest **3** .... (increase) our marketing budget this year by about 20%. I think we will have **4** .... (spend) more on advertising in order **5** .... (raise) brand awareness. Competition in our sector has been increasing, and we have to avoid **6** .... (lose) market share to our competitors, which is something we risk **7** .... (do) by **8** .... (follow) our present strategy. Also, by **9** .... (contact) our main customers directly, we may be able **10** .... (find out) why our products are losing competitiveness. I think it would be worth **11** .... (do) this, and also **12** .... (think) about **13** .... (develop) new lines and **14** .... (innovate) a bit more. Perhaps we could arrange **15** .... (meet) sometime **16** .... (discuss) this. I would be happy **17** .... (see) you any time next week.

Looking forward to **18** .... (hear) from you,

Vince

Writing

Write a short reply to Vince's email above.
• Agree to a meeting.
• Explain why it may be difficult to increase the budget.
• Suggest a suitable time.

6 Launching a product

Vocabulary

1 Complete this table with the missing word forms.

verb	noun	adjective
1 *found*	founder	
	entrepreneur	**2**
	skill	**3**
commute	**4**	
launch	**5**	
establish	**6**	**7**
opt	**8**	**9**
rely	**10**	**11**
distribute	**12**	

2 Choose the correct answer – A, B or C.

1 A luxury product which is high quality and expensive is a(n) ......*A*...... product.
   A **upmarket**   B downmarket   C middle-market

2 A product which only appeals to a very specialist group of customers is a .... product.
   A special   B niche   C reserved

3 The percentage of the market which your company has is your market ....
   A quota   B segment   C share

4 What is a brand called which has the supermarket's name on it?
   A an own brand   B a white brand   C a proprietary brand

5 Which word has these three meanings: *start (a company), put (a product) on the market, start (an advertising campaign)*?
   A throw   B begin   C launch

6 What do marketers call the place where the product reaches the consumer?
   A an end-user   B a final stop   C an outlet

7 What is another word for direct mail?
   A correspondence   B junk mail   C snail mail

8 When a company subsidises a football team or a music concert, what is this called?
   A endorsement   B subvention   C sponsorship

9 Which of these publicity materials is likely to look like a colour magazine?
   A a brochure   B a leaflet   C a newsletter

Grammar and writing

1 You work in the marketing department of Turbodrinks. Study these charts which show Turbodrinks' spending on promotion of their energy bar. Complete the sentences below by writing a preposition in each gap.

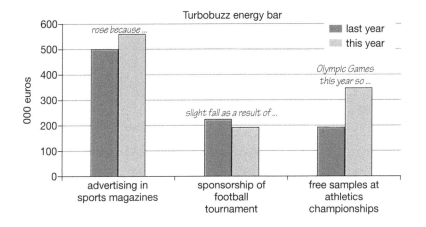

Turbobuzz energy bar

- rose because …
- Olympic Games this year so …
- slight fall as a result of …

last year / this year

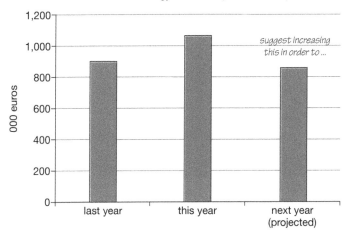

Turbobuzz energy bar – total promotional spend

- suggest increasing this in order to …

1 Our spending on advertising in sports magazines has risen ......*by*...... €50,000 .... €550,000.

2 We have reduced the amount we spend .... football sponsorship .... €230,000 .... €180,000.

3 Our spending .... free samples at athletics championships this year has been €350,000, an increase .... €170,000 .... last year.

2 Now use both the charts and all the handwritten notes to write a brief report for your manager.

7 A stand at a trade fair

Vocabulary

1 How many compound nouns can you make by combining a word from box A with a word from box B?

Example: *exhibition organisers*

A

| customer   floor   furniture   event |
| exhibition   export   publicity |

B

| base   centre   exhibition   markets |
| material   organisers   space   stand |

2 Complete each of these sentences with a compound noun from Exercise 1.

1 Can you contact the *exhibition organisers* to find out how much it would cost to exhibit?

2 How long does it take to get from the airport to the .... ?

3 I'd prefer to hire an .... rather buy than custom-build one because we don't have room to store it when it's not in use.

4 It's a good opportunity to meet foreign buyers and have a chance to open new ....

5 We shall need about 40 square metres of .... for our stand.

6 We try to expand our .... by exhibiting at trade fairs.

7 We will need quite a lot of shelves for all our .... , such as leaflets, catalogues and brochures.

Writing

1 Complete this email by writing one word in each gap.

Dear Sir/Madam

1 ...*We*... are a medium-sized business based in Riga, Latvia, specialising
2 .... the development and production of marine electronic instruments. We are interested in the possibility **3** .... marketing our products in your country and are contacting companies in the sector **4** .... might be willing to act as agents or distributors for **5** .... products. We wonder **6** .... you would be interested in acting in this role for us. I **7** .... be visiting your country during the first fortnight of next month and would welcome the chance of a meeting with you.
8 .... you suggest a day and a time **9** .... would be convenient for you?
I look **10** .... to hearing from you.
Brigita Skuja
Export Sales Director

2 **Your boss has asked you to write a reply to the email in Exercise 1.**
  Write the email:
  - saying that you would be interested in acting as agents
  - saying that your boss would like a meeting
  - suggesting a day and a time.

  Write 40–50 words.

Reading

There is one extra word in every numbered line of this email. Cross out the extra words.

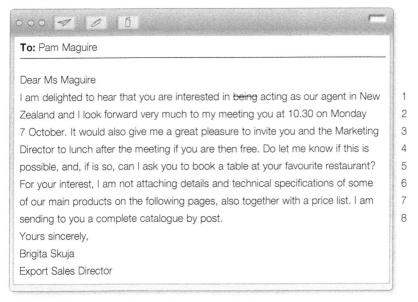

To: Pam Maguire	
Dear Ms Maguire	
I am delighted to hear that you are interested in ~~being~~ acting as our agent in New	1
Zealand and I look forward very much to my meeting you at 10.30 on Monday	2
7 October. It would also give me a great pleasure to invite you and the Marketing	3
Director to lunch after the meeting if you are then free. Do let me know if this is	4
possible, and, if is so, can I ask you to book a table at your favourite restaurant?	5
For your interest, I am not attaching details and technical specifications of some	6
of our main products on the following pages, also together with a price list. I am	7
sending to you a complete catalogue by post.	8
Yours sincerely,	
Brigita Skuja	
Export Sales Director	

Grammar

Complete these formal requests by writing one word in each gap.

1 Can you please ....*tell*.... me how much floor space .... per metre at the
  exhibition?

2 We .... appreciate it .... you could send us details of hotels in the
  area which offer discounts.

3 I would be very .... if you .... give me information on the other
  companies exhibiting at the show.

4 I wonder .... you could let me .... what time the exhibition opens and
  closes to the public.

5 We would be pleased if .... could inform us about .... to obtain
  complimentary entrance tickets for our clients.

8 Being persuasive

Vocabulary

1 **Choose the correct way of saying these figures.**

1 535
   A five hundred thirty-five   B five hundred and thirty-five
2 233,499
   A two hundred, thirty-three thousand, four hundred, ninety-nine
   B two hundred and thirty-three thousand, four hundred and ninety-nine
3 2.5
   A two point five   B two and five
4 10.25
   A ten point twenty-five   B ten point two five
5 50%
   A a fifty per cent   B fifty per cent
6 £3.50
   A three pounds fifty   B three fifty pounds
7 €19.99
   A nineteen euros ninety-nine   B nineteen euros and ninety-nine
8 €45,000 p.a.
   A forty-five thousand euros a year
   B forty and five thousand euros a year

2 **Complete the paragraph below with words or phrases from the box.**
Where necessary, check the meanings in your dictionary.

> bulk orders   discount   mark-up   ~~overheads~~   profit margin
> recommended retail price   reductions

We are a small agricultural business which produces oranges for the export
market. Our 1 _overheads_, or routine costs, such as water for irrigation or
pesticides, are pretty high. This means that when we sell our products, our
2 .... is very narrow. Also, we face a lot of competition, so when buyers
place 3 .... , they often expect a hefty 4 .... or 5 .... in price.
Some years, there's no profit at all. On the other hand, when you go to the
supermarket, you see that the same fruit has been given an enormous 6 ....
– sometimes as much as 400% – and the 7 .... bears no relation to the
price we were given when we sold the oranges.

Grammar

Complete these first or second conditional sentences by writing the verbs in brackets in the correct tenses.

1 I'd give you a 15% discount on condition that you _paid_ (pay) us within 30 days.

2 We .... (not be) able to stay in business unless he pays in cash.

3 We .... (place) an order for 50,000 units, providing you were able to get them to us in time for the start of our promotional campaign.

4 As long as you .... (guarantee) that we would be your sole supplier, we .... (allow) you to have the goods at a special price.

5 Unless you pay the full price, we .... (not manage) to cover our overheads.

6 Unless the goods .... (arrive) next week, they .... (be) late for the beginning of the season.

7 We .... (offer) them a better deal if they .... (be) more reliable customers, but they're not.

Reading

Read this email. There is an extra word in every numbered line.
Cross out the extra words.

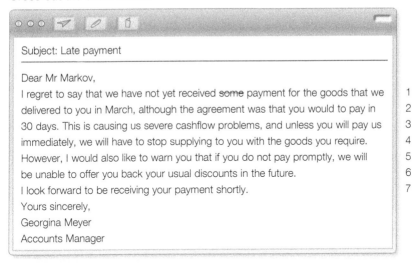

Subject: Late payment

Dear Mr Markov,
I regret to say that we have not yet received ~~some~~ payment for the goods that we   1
delivered to you in March, although the agreement was that you would to pay in   2
30 days. This is causing us severe cashflow problems, and unless you will pay us   3
immediately, we will have to stop supplying to you with the goods you require.   4
However, I would also like to warn you that if you do not pay promptly, we will   5
be unable to offer you back your usual discounts in the future.   6
I look forward to be receiving your payment shortly.   7
Yours sincerely,
Georgina Meyer
Accounts Manager

Writing

You received the above email this morning. Write an email to your assistant telling him to:
• investigate the cause of the problem
• pay the invoice
• apologise and explain to Ms Meyer.

You should write about 40–50 words.

Starting a business

Vocabulary

1 Match the words and phrases (1–9) with their definitions (a–i).

1 concept   a   the total income a company receives

2 gross revenue   b   a loan to buy a house

3 entrepreneur   c   an idea

4 outlet   d   money you get from the company when you lose your job

5 supply chain   e   the system of people and organisations that are involved in getting a product from the place where it is made to customers

6 redundancy money   f   selling through a shop

7 mortgage   g   shop or other place where a company sells its products

8 retail   h   someone who starts a business

9 investor   i   someone who puts money into a business in order to make a profit

2 a Look at the words in the box below and say which word refers to the …

1 organisation which gives franchises

2 person or company which receives a franchise licence.

franchiser   franchisee

b Make similar pairs of words from these verbs.

1 employ   2 interview   3 train   4 pay

3 Complete the sentences below with the words in the box.

assets   costs   liabilities   profits   rate   tax   ~~turnover~~

1 Another word for total sales is *turnover* .

2 Factories and other property are fixed ....

3 Our debts are ....

4 Our pre-tax .... are up by 25% this year.

5 Salaries have risen, which means that staff .... are higher.

6 The interest .... is 6.5%.

7 We have to pay a .... on profits of 25%.

4 Put the correct form of *do, make* or *go* in each gap.

My dream is to **1** ...*make*.. as much money as possible as quickly as possible, and I believe that the only way to **2** .... this is to speculate. Basically, speculating is **3** .... investments when things are cheap, then hoping they will **4** .... up in price very quickly, then selling. It's not the same as **5** .... a job, of course, and you need some capital to start with. Also, there's the risk that you will lose your investment and **6** .... bankrupt. On the other hand, if you have the money, it's easier than **7** .... into business, but perhaps less satisfying.

Grammar

Complete these emails by writing a preposition in each gap. In some cases, more than one answer is possible.

Hi Bruno
Silvie wants to have a meeting **1** .....*on*..... Friday **2** .... 3 p.m. Can you make it?
I have another meeting which will probably go on **3** .... 2.30, so it looks like I'm going to miss lunch unless we can put it back **4** .... 3.30. What do you think?
Carmen

Paco,
I know you were in charge of ordering the company calendar **5** .... at least four years. This is now my responsibility. Am I right in thinking you ordered it **6** ....
August of the previous year and they normally delivered it **7** .... the end of October **8** .... the latest?
Sergio

Fu,
Could you order a limousine **9** .... five o'clock to pick up our visitors from the airport? Also, I think we should put them up at the Hilton **10** .... their stay. Could you please book that, too? I see they've been good customers of ours
11 .... 1995, so **12** .... nearly 20 years. We should really treat them well to show we appreciate them.
Thanks
May

Writing

You are an office manager. An important client is visiting the office this week for a meeting. Write an email to your assistant asking her to:
• book a taxi from the station and saying what time
• arrange a meeting room (with times)
• book a table at a restaurant (with time).

Vocabulary

1 Read this text about someone who joined a franchise called Petpals, which looks after people's domestic animals while they are working or on holiday. Choose the best answer – A, B, C or D – to fill each gap.

Brendan Humphrey of Petpals Winchester says, 'I **1** .....*D*..... my £40,000-a-year job as a surveyor to join the franchise, **2** .... up all the associated stress, and I have not **3** .... a single moment of the old job.

It was hard work for the first year, as I was **4** .... my business and we had to be **5** .... with money, but what a great year! I could not believe it; in our first year, our turnover **6** .... just over £35,000, producing around £10,000 **7** .... profit, and we even managed to **8** .... most of our finance. No more stresses and strains of the old life, I have lost weight, have peace of mind, sanity and I'm doing a **9** .... I wouldn't change for anything.' Petpals Winchester now **10** .... four part-time assistants and is growing at a controlled **11** .... of around 20% a quarter.

Part of a famous rock band that started back in the sixties, Richard Herd, of Petpals Saffron Walden, wanted a business that he could **12** .... with his wife, Pauline. That would allow them to work together in harmony while **13** .... a rewarding service to busy pet owners. Richard and Pauline say, 'We enjoy being very much part of the franchise. Support is always on **14** .... if we need it.'

1	A stopped	B threw	C went	D quit
2	A leaving	B giving	C throwing	D stopping
3	A lost	B mislaid	C missed	D longed
4	A growing	B doing	C looking	D working
5	A careful	B cautious	C tight	D short
6	A arrived	B reached	C rose	D met
7	A complete	B large	C gross	D top
8	A pay up	B pay in	C pay out	D pay off
9	A contract	B business	C job	D work
10	A employs	B contracts	C engages	D hires
11	A amount	B percentage	C number	D rate
12	A work	B run	C do	D make
13	A sending	B paying	C providing	D renting
14	A hand	B paper	C reach	D side

2 Complete the sentences below, containing advice about starting a business, with words or phrases from the box.

| ~~assets~~ borrow business plan cashflow collateral investors loan market rate |
| market research overheads tax returns |

1 Use _assets_ such as your house or any other property you have as .... in order to raise a .... from the bank.

2 Check that they are not asking you to pay interest above the .... and be ready to show them your .... to demonstrate that you have a reasonable income.

3 Carry out .... to make sure there are customers for your product or services and that you will have enough income to cover your .... and maintain your ....

4 Write a .... that will convince banks or other .... that your idea is sound.

5 Above all, don't .... more than you can repay.

Writing

1 Complete this letter by putting one word in each gap.

Dear Mr Allen,

Thank you **1** _for_ your letter of 14 June in **2** .... you apply for a Young Entrepreneur's Grant to help you set **3** .... your business.

We would be very happy **4** .... consider your application and in any case offer **5** .... advice which you may find useful. We would like to invite you to **6** .... interview where we can discuss your application **7** .... Monday 1 July.

Please telephone me to **8** .... me know if the date is convenient or, if **9** .... , to arrange a different **10** ....

Yours sincerely,

Gudrun Lear

2 Your boss has received a letter from a student called Mary Hall, who would like to gain work experience with your company. He has asked you to write a letter in reply in which you should:
  • invite Ms Hall for an interview
  • say when and where the interview will be held
  • ask her to phone you to confirm the time.

Use the letter in Exercise 1 as a model.

11 Expanding into Europe

Vocabulary

1 **Circle the odd word out in each set.**

1 secretary   PA   (CEO)   typist
2 headquarters   head office   branch   HQ
3 warehouse   stockroom   showroom   storeroom
4 shop floor   boardroom   factory   production facility
5 facility   shop   outlet   store
6 the board   shareholders   management   directors
7 back office   research facility   laboratory   R&D
8 develop   innovate   modify   launch

2 a **Combine words in box A with words in box B to make compound nouns or adjectives.**

Example: *cold calling*

A

B

| cold   cost   eye   ground   job   knowledge |
| problem   record   team   time |

| breaking   building   calling   catching |
| consuming   cutting   sharing   solving |

b **Use the compound nouns to complete these sentences.**

1 Phoning a potential client whom you have never spoken to before –
cold calling – is the part of my job I like least.

2 He only wants to work part time, so he's interested in a ....
arrangement with someone else in the office.

3 I find a lot of this paperwork very .... , which is frustrating and
stops me getting on with more vital work.

4 In our laboratories in South Africa, we're doing some .... , totally
innovative research.

5 The main purpose of this meeting is .... , so that at the end of the
meeting, we'll all have told each other what we know about the latest
marketing techniques.

6 A lot of you haven't worked together before, so before we start on the
project, we're going to do some .... activities together.

7 The company is doing some .... by relocating headquarters out of
the centre of town to a cheaper area.

8 The purpose of this brainstorming session is to think of some ....
ideas to get us out of our present difficulties.

9 The shareholders are really happy this year because our company has
made .... profits.

10 We need .... displays of our best products in our showroom.

Reading

Read this proposal. There is one wrong word in every line. Cross out the wrong word and write the correct word.

Proposal for launching our products in Eastern Europe

Introduction

The purpose ~~for~~ this proposal is to suggest that we market our products   1 *of*
in Europe and to present a plot of action.   2

Current situation

In present, our main markets are Africa, North America and East Asia.   3
Although, despite the economic problems that many countries in   4
Europe are suffering from, we believe that it is a region who offers our   5
company a major opportunity to expansion and growth.   6

Market research

Initially, it should be a good idea to carry out market research to find out: 7
• who our competitors will become in the market   8
• which prices customers would be prepared to pay   9
• which retail shops would be suitable and willing to sell our products.   10

Finding an agent or distributor

I suggested we place an advertisement in a trade journal in each of   11
the target countries, inviting potential agents or distributors to do   12
contact with us. Members of the marketing band should then visit the countries   13
and meet the agents in time to assess which would be the most suitable.   14

Conclusion

I recommend that we should start investigating this markets   15
straightaway and aim to put our products in those countries in   16
between six months to the year. The finance department should   17
also set aside a budget in this activity.   18

Grammar

Join these sentences using the words in brackets. Write your answers in your notebook.

1 He's very competent. He never got promotion. (*despite*)
   Despite being very competent, he never got promotion.
2 They had a large budget. They ran short of money. (*although*)
3 We carried out market research. Our product failed. (*in spite of*)
4 The company was extremely successful. It had cashflow problems. (*although*)
5 We decided to rent the premises. The premises were extremely expensive.
   (*despite*)
6 Our agent didn't understand the market. He was a local man. (*although*)
7 We spent over £1m on advertising. Brand awareness didn't improve.
   (*in spite of*)

12 Presenting your business idea

Vocabulary

1 Match the pieces of equipment in the box to their descriptions (1–8) below.

> data projector   flipchart   ~~handouts~~   laptop   pointer   remote control
> product samples   screen

1 These are often photocopies. You can include complex information which is difficult to explain and hand them out to people. *handouts*
2 This is a computer you can carry around, so it's great for taking to a presentation.
3 This is where you can project your charts and slides so that everyone in the room can see them.
4 You can hand these round so people can actually handle and see what you are talking about.
5 You can operate equipment from anywhere in the room using this.
6 You can use this to point at things on the screen, and a little red light will shine where you point it.
7 You can use this to show information from a computer on a large screen.
8 You can write notes on these large pages before your lecture and just turn them over when you need them. Also, you can write here during your talk.

2 Match the sentence beginnings (1–9) with the sentence endings (a–i) to make typical signalling phrases for presentations.

1 Good afternoon and

2 Thank you for
3 Let me introduce myself:
4 What I would like to do in this presentation is
5 My presentation will have four parts.
6 If you have any questions while I'm speaking,
7 Now, I'd like to conclude by
8 Finally, let me finish by saying
9 Now if you have any other questions, I'd

a describe this company to you and outline our business plans for the next year.
b don't hesitate to interrupt me.
c finding the time to come today.
d be happy to answer them.
e my name's Fatima Belenguer.
f summarising my main points again.
g that it's been a pleasure talking to you, and thank you for your time.
h The first part will be to tell you what our company does.
i welcome to the offices of Quickinvest Ltd.

Grammar

1 Read this extract from a presentation and put the verbs in brackets into the correct form.

> Good morning, and welcome to the Adelphi Hotel. Thank you all very much for
> I _coming_ (come); some of you **2** .... (travel) a long way **3** .... (hear) us
> today, and I hope you **4** .... (all have) good journeys. So let me **5** ....
> (introduce) myself: my name's Peter Furlong, and this is my partner, Mark Davies.
> The purpose of this presentation is **6** .... (explain) our business plans to
> you and hopefully to get you interested in **7** .... (invest) in Clock Options
> Express.
> In my presentation, I **8** .... (aim) to do three things. First, I **9** .... (give)
> you a short summary of our main business idea. Then I **10** .... (tell) you
> the findings of the market research that we **11** .... (conduct), and finally I
> **12** .... (outline) our financial requirements and plans, which should show
> you what a sound and exciting investment Clock Options Express **13** ....
> (represent). If you have any questions you **14** .... (like) to ask, I **15** ....
> (be) happy **16** .... (answer) them at the end of the talk.

2 Complete these sentences with *can* or *could*. In one sentence, both words are possible.

1 When we first opened the offices here, we _could_ find parking spaces very easily. Now, it's almost impossible.

2 Be careful of Franz. He .... get very irritable if you interrupt him when he's busy.

3 I don't know what has happened to Maria – she's not usually late. I suppose she .... be in a meeting.

4 If you have difficulty concentrating in the office, you .... take the work home to complete there – I don't mind.

5 Hello. I don't think we've met before. How .... I help you?

6 I'd be grateful if you .... chair the meeting today, as I have a sore throat.

7 Now that you've completed the training course, I'm sure you .... deal with customers without me supervising you.

Vocabulary and writing

1 Complete this letter by choosing the most appropriate word – A, B, C or D – for each gap.

Dear Sirs,

Please **1** ...*B*... a double room for me for the nights **2** .... 18 and 19 March.

If possible, I would like the room to be in a quiet **3** .... of the hotel.

I shall **4** .... to meet a **5** .... of clients on the morning of 20 March, **6** .... could you make a meeting room **7** .... for me on that day from 9 a.m. to 2 p.m.?

I do not **8** .... to arrive until about 11 p.m. on 18 March, so please **9** .... my room for me. As I will be hungry after my **10** .... from Mannheim, could you tell me if the restaurant will still be **11** .... at that time?

Also, please email me as soon as possible to **12** .... that these bookings have been made. If you **13** .... me to send a deposit in **14** .... , let me know and I shall be **15** .... to do so.

Yours faithfully,

1 A hold	B reserve	C get	D give
2 A on	B of	C for	D in
3 A place	B space	C part	D section
4 A like	B prefer	C need	D think
5 A quantity	B number	C selection	D range
6 A then	B and	C so	D therefore
7 A suitable	B free	C empty	D available
8 A expect	B hope	C think	D anticipate
9 A have	B reserve	C maintain	D keep
10 A trip	B travel	C journey	D arrival
11 A served	B open	C opened	D providing
12 A ensure	B promise	C confirm	D agree
13 A demand	B require	C hope	D oblige
14 A ahead	B advance	C preparation	D priority
15 A wanting	B ready	C prepared	D glad

2 Look at this hotel webpage. Using all the handwritten notes, write an email to the hotel to make a booking.

River Hotel, Wroclaw

Situated in the old town with views across the river, the River Hotel offers a comfortable, convenient and stylish stay. The restaurant offers the best in traditional Polish cuisine.

For business travellers, the hotel has a fully equipped business centre, together with meeting and conference rooms.

Make the River Hotel your business centre during your stay.

Book rooms for team – say how many

With views please!

Breakfast included?

Will need these – give details and enquire about prices

Grammar

1 Complete these sentences by putting the verbs in brackets into the correct forms.

1 The plane was delayed, and they didn't tell us. They *should have told* (*should/tell*) us as soon as they knew.

2 I thought the aircraft was pretty dirty. They .... (*should/clean*) it properly before we got on board.

3 They allowed the economy-class passengers to board first. I think they .... (*should/allow*) the business-class passengers to go first.

4 The steward gave me the same food as the economy-class passengers. I think he .... (*should/give*) me better food.

5 We had to queue to get off the plane. We .... (*should/not/have*) to queue.

2 Complete these sentences in your notebook in any way you like using the form *should have* + past participle.
1 There was nobody waiting for me at the airport. They …
2 The bank was closed when I arrived, so I couldn't change money. The bank …
3 The customs officer was rude when he searched my luggage. He …
4 It took over an hour for my luggage to come through to the baggage reclaim. They …

Vocabulary

1 **Match these phrasal verbs (1–10) from the Student's Book unit and the transcripts with their definitions (a–j).**

1	come up with	a	arrange a meeting or event
2	deal with	b	collect someone or something
3	follow up	c	get information about something
4	cut off	d	give or find an explanation for something
5	clear up	e	start a new activity
6	pick up	f	stop or interrupt
7	find out	g	suggest or think of an idea or plan
8	note down	h	take action in order to achieve something or solve a problem
9	move on	i	take further action connected with someone or something
10	fix up	j	write something down so you don't forget it

2 **Complete these sentences by writing the correct form of a phrasal verb from Exercise 1 in each gap. In some sentences, more than one phrasal verb is possible.**

1 Fortunately the bank *has come up with* a very satisfactory solution to our financial problems.

2 I don't know the answer, but I can .... for you.

3 I'll just .... your email address in my notebook and I'll get back to you when I'm in the office.

4 I'm sorry I had to .... the conversation, but I had an urgent call on the other line.

5 I've been in the same job for three years and I feel it's time to .... and do something new.

6 Maria is trying to .... a meeting with the Koreans for after our visit to China next month.

7 Pachi will .... the visitors .... from the airport and take them to their hotel.

8 We managed to .... all the misunderstandings in quite a short meeting.

9 Yoshio gave us a very useful contact and when we .... it .... , we were able to do some very profitable business.

10 You need to speak to Malik – he's the one who .... customer queries and can give you an answer.

3 **Write the opposites of these adjectives.**

1 usual   *unusual*   5 reliable   ....
2 persuasive   .... 6 organised   ....
3 proven   .... 7 communicative   ....
4 motivating   ....

4 **Complete this table. In many cases, more than one word is possible. Think of as many as you can.**

noun	verb	adjective
1 *persuasion, persuasiveness*	persuade	**2** *persuasive*
3	implement	
4	consult	**5**
6	exhibit	
7	present	
8	operate	**9**
10	prove	**11**
12	combine	**13**
14	finance	**15**
16	motivate	**17**
18	rely	**19**
20	organise	**21**
22	communicate	**23**

5 **Complete these sentences with the adjectives from Exercise 4 (either positive or negative).**

1 He was an extremely *persuasive* speaker, and we all found ourselves agreeing with him.

2 Sheila is so .... that you never know if she will do the job properly or not.

3 I find that, for a salesman, Brian is surprisingly .... and he never really tells you if there are problems or not. You have to find them out for yourself.

4 The conference could have been better .... A lot of the sessions started in chaos.

5 He's an excellent speaker with a .... track record.

6 It's very .... after all the preparation to find that only seven people came to my talk.

15 Business meetings

Vocabulary

1 Use the words in the box to complete the note below.

> action   agenda   ~~attend~~   chair(person)   circulate   minutes

---

Amanda,

I've got to **1** *attend* an important meeting of the Advisory Board tomorrow.
Could you:

* find out who is going to be the **2** ....
* get hold of the **3** .... for me so I can prepare – and make sure you
  4 .... it to the other members of the board
* check that the **5** .... of the last meeting are typed up
* come in for 20 minutes after lunch so we can check that all the **6** ....
  points have been followed up?

Thanks

Sarah

---

2 a Match the words on the left (1–5) with with the words on the right (a–e)
to make compound nouns which describe reasons for having meetings.

1 brain   a building
2 decision   b making
3 information   c solving
4 problem   d sharing
5 team   e storming

b Complete these sentences using the compounds.

1 Later today, we'll be holding a *brainstorming* session to get ideas for new
  promotional activities.
2 I know many of you think that email is a more efficient way of .... ,
  but I can't be sure you read all your emails, so I thought I'd take this
  opportunity to tell you a few things.
3 Quite a number of the people have never worked together before, so the
  prime purpose of the meeting this afternoon is ....
4 We've discussed the issues at length on other occasions, so this meeting
  is primarily a .... meeting where we shall be taking the company in
  a new direction.
5 A number of difficulties have arisen in the production department, so
  today we're having a .... meeting to see if we can sort them out.

3 **Complete this crossword using verbs from page 70 of the Student's Book.**

Across

1 I've got too much work on my plate, so I think I'll ....*skip*.... this afternoon's meeting.

3 I've decided to .... the meeting because it's not really necessary. (4, 3)

4 Who's going to .... today's meeting? You, Malik?

6 You're all looking pretty tired, so let's .... till after lunch.

7 If you don't .... the meeting, you won't know what decisions are being taken.

Down

2 Katya is ill, so I think we should .... the meeting until she's back at work. (3,3)

3 We need to .... the agenda before the meeting so that people can think about the issues.

5 Where are we going to .... the meeting? In the boardroom?

Grammar

Replace the underlined words/phrases with pronouns in this memo to staff to avoid repetition.

there

The last meeting we held was very frustrating because no one who was **1** at the meeting came prepared for **2** the meeting. The **3** meeting last week was better because at least everyone knew what was on the agenda. However, **4** the meeting was too short for some of the participants to get to know **5** the other participants. **6** The fact that it was too short meant that none of **7** the participants was happy with the decisions we took.

Could you all in future organise meetings better and come prepared? Many thanks.

16 Spending the sales budget

Vocabulary

1 For each gap, choose the best word – A, B, C or D.

Introduction

The **1** ...C... of this report is to summarise the performance of the Burjassot Sports Centre this year and its projected performance in the **2** .... year.

Use of sports centre

The **3** .... of days that the sports centre is used has **4** .... by approximately 15% this year, from 310 to 362, **5** .... to the fact that it now opens on Sundays. This situation is projected to continue next year as well.

6 .... , the number of members using the sports centre each day has fallen: last year, there was an **7** .... of 163 people per day, whereas the average was just 148 this year. However, this figure is **8** .... to recover next year to approximately 160.

Financial performance

Turnover rose from just **9** .... £5m last year to £5.5m this year, and this positive **10** .... is expected to continue next year. Profits also rose **11** .... this year. They increased by approximately £150,000 from £540,000 to £690,000. Moreover, this figure is forecast to rise even **12** .... to about £800,000 next year.

Conclusion

Our level of activity is **13** .... and our financial performance is **14** .... healthy. Next year, we may consider **15** .... some of the profits in renovating the installations.

---

1 A motive	B reason	C purpose	D thinking
2 A coming	B subsequent	C following	D next
3 A figure	B number	C amount	D total
4 A risen	B raised	C boomed	D put up
5 A due	B because	C consequence	D explained
6 A Although	B Whereas	C While	D However
7 A account	B estimate	C amount	D average
8 A forecast	B hoped	C planned	D thought
9 A under	B underneath	C less	D fewer
10 A tendency	B fashion	C trend	D direction
11 A meaningfully	B significantly	C emphatically	D especially
12 A greater	B longer	C further	D larger
13 A enhancing	B increasing	C boosting	D overtaking
14 A absolutely	B greatly	C extremely	D highly
15 A reinvesting	B returning	C reserving	D repaying

2 Decide whether each of these words expresses an increase (I) or a decrease (D).

1 cut *D*
2 drop
3 fall

4 go down
5 go up
6 plummet

7 raise
8 recover
9 reduce

10 rise
11 soar
12 rocket

3 Study this chart and complete the description below using words from Exercise 2.

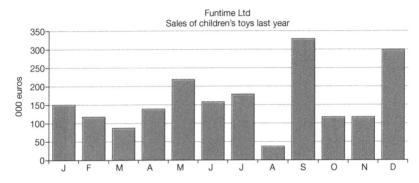

Funtime Ltd
Sales of children's toys last year

Sales of children's toys **1** *dropped* from €150,000 in January to €90,000 in March. Then they **2** .... to reach €220,000 in May before **3** .... again to €160,000 in June. In July, they **4** .... slightly to €170,000 before **5** .... to €40,000 in August. In September, sales **6** .... to €330,000 and then **7** .... to €120,000 for October and November. In December, they **8** .... once again to €300,000.

Grammar

Put the verbs in brackets into the correct form of the passive.

Nonstop Watches **1** *was started* (start) in 1968 by Ian Murray from a small workshop in his garden in Dundee. Its first product, a waterproof stopwatch, **2** .... (launch) the same year and was an immediate success when it **3** .... (adopt) as the official stopwatch for the 1968 Highland Games. In 1969, the company moved to a factory just outside Dundee, and in that factory, more than five million watches **4** .... (produce) until now. In a constant bid for innovation, the latest digital technology **5** .... (recently introduce) to make Nonstop Watches among the most accurate and reliable in the world, and these watches **6** .... (expect) **7** .... (use) as the official watches at the next Commonwealth Games. Next year, it **8** .... (hope) that a new completely automated factory **9** .... (open) and that all watches coming from the factory **10** .... (manufacture) by robots.

Vocabulary

Complete these sentences by writing a verb which collocates with the noun in bold in the correct form.

1 We _missed_ an excellent **opportunity** to sound out some customers' opinions. What a pity!
2 Using social media is an excellent way of .... in **contact** with younger consumers.
3 The company .... a bad **mistake** when it denied that there was anything wrong with the product.
4 As a management consultant, part of my job is to .... **recommendations** on efficiency.
5 We have .... a huge amount of market **research** in the past year.
6 Only three people .... the **meeting**, so it was rather a failure.
7 He has a reputation for reliability and .... his **deadlines**.
8 Now that we've decided on the **changes**, we just need to .... them.
9 The airline has just .... an **order** for 30 new aircraft.
10 I'd like to .... a **suggestion** if I may concerning your website.

Grammar

Complete the text by writing *the* or – (where you think no article is needed) in each gap.

What the Web taught FedEx

To understand how thoroughly **1** ...*the*.... Web has permeated **2** .... everyday business life, think back to **3** .... last time you tracked a package. Maybe you typed www.fedex.com into your browser. Or maybe you just pulled up **4** .... shipment information from **5** .... retailer's website.

That act, so normal today, was revolutionary when FedEx first introduced **6** .... online package tracking. In its early days, **7** .... company internet sites were a sea of static corporate brochures, with **8** .... messages from CEOs displayed on **9** .... grey pages. **10** .... idea that you could use it for something that actually touched **11** .... real world was unheard of. **12** .... Internet has greatly increased **13** .... number of contacts **14** .... customers have with FedEx. But it's also cut **15** .... costs for **16** .... company by $45 million a month, since an online tracking request costs 2 cents, vs. $2.40 for a phone call.

Reading

Read this email. In most lines, there is one wrong word. Cross out the wrong word and write the correct word. If you think the line is correct, put a tick (✓).

To: Frank Lenz	
Cc: Marina Laporte	
Subject: Upgrading our website	
Hello Frank	
Recently ~~us~~ company sales have been increasing quite rapidly here in Europe,	1 *our*
and for a result of our use of social media, we are receiving enquiries from customers	2
in another parts of the world as well. These represent a business opportunity	3
what we ought to take advantage of.	4
We discuss this issue at a meeting of marketing personnel yesterday and decided	5
that we should set off a facility for online sales. We also decided that our social media	6
pages should be available in other languages apart of English and French. We thought	7
that they should also be translated into Spanish and Chinese.	8
Could it be possible for you to adapt our pages in the ways I have suggested, and	9
could you give me a quotation for how much it would cost to carry on this work?	10
If you require further informations, please call me on 964 538729 (direct line).	11
Best wishes	
Nicole Crété	

Writing

Your company or the place where you study is deciding whether it needs to use the Internet and social media differently. Your director has asked you to write a report on how your company/college uses these things at the moment and any changes that are needed.

Write your report for your director describing how the Internet and social media are used by the company/college at the moment.

Write about:
* how useful these media are
* how well they are being used
* any improvements you can suggest.

You can use the reports in the Writing reference of the Student's Book on page 121 as models.

Vocabulary

1 **Complete these sentences by writing *method(s)* or *way(s)* in each gap.**

1 Our environmental-impact measurement *methods* are highly complex and amongst the most advanced and reliable in the world.

2 One .... to reduce our power consumption would be to install low-energy light bulbs.

3 Our company could become more environmentally friendly in several ...., including increased recycling of paper and using electric cars.

4 The company's accounting .... need to be updated to meet the new financial regulations.

2 **Choose the right word – A, B, C or D – for each gap.**

1 Environmental problems are ....*A*...... the way many companies do business.

   A affecting   B impacting   C reviewing   D reorganising

2 By careful management, companies can .... resources.

   A reduce   B cut   C save   D drop

3 Leaving your computer on all night .... power.

   A burns   B wastes   C employs   D spends

4 Printers and other devices will be used in offices for the .... future.

   A predictable   B forecast   C foretold   D foreseeable

5 One .... you can take to reduce your environmental impact is to recycle paper.

   A way   B method   C measure   D means

6 One .... of modern computers is that if they are left idle for some time, they automatically switch to standby mode.

   A trend   B feature   C factor   D speciality

7 The new machinery has enabled us to .... our production process while being more environmentally friendly.

   A speed   B boost   C streamline   D quicken

8 We're hoping our new waste-recycling plant will attract corporate ....

   A investors   B spenders   C savers   D speculators

9 This machine never breaks down – in fact, it's the most .... one in the factory.

   A trustworthy   B trusted   C faithful   D reliable

10 Our staff are totally .... on reducing our carbon footprint and making the company the greenest in the sector.

   A determined   B focused   C committed   D convinced

Grammar

1 Complete the extract below from a report by writing a word or phrase from the box in each gap.

> because   due to   owing   result   the fact that   why

> Our electricity bill has rocketed **1** *because* of the price increase introduced
> last January, so it is essential to find savings in electricity costs. The office is
> often too hot in the winter due to **2** .... the heating is turned up too high.
> Moreover, a lot of energy is wasted **3** .... people opening the windows
> to cool down. In summer, on the other hand, **4** .... to the powerful air
> conditioning, some people come to work dressed in warm clothes, and it may be
> the reason **5** .... many of them suffer from colds in the summer. Addressing
> these problems would **6** .... in a significant reduction in our overheads.

2 Complete these sentences to make predictions about offices of the future. Give a reason for each prediction.

1 It's quite likely that in the next 20 years, computers ...
   It's quite likely that in the next 20 years, computers will do all routine office work due to improved software.
2 There's a chance that in the future, office workers ...
3 The energy consumed in offices is bound ...
4 The offices of the future are unlikely ...
5 Computer software in the future may possibly be able to ...
6 Offices in the future will probably be ...

Writing

The office where you work or your college is considering ways of reducing its environmental impact. Your line manager has asked you to suggest ways in which this can be done.

Write a short proposal:
* explaining what things in the office are having a negative environmental impact
* outlining ways the office can reduce its environmental impact
* explaining any other benefits from these measures
* saying which measures you favour.

19 A staff survey

Vocabulary

1 Complete the text below with a word or phrase from the box.

absenteeism   bonus scheme   long hours   motivated   off sick   productivity
staff retention   staff turnover   work–life

Making staff happy

May Electronics had a problem of **1** *absenteeism* , with many staff phoning in to say they were sick. Also, although they paid high wages, workers did not seem to stay with them long, and **2** .... was almost 20% a year. Eventually, the Managing Director, Sophie May, decided to call in a consultant, who reached the conclusion that most staff were under too much stress. Many complained that they worked **3** .... and that, as a result, they were unable to have a reasonable **4** .... balance. Also, many felt that management did not value their work, and, as a result, they did not feel **5** .... to work very hard. The fact that workers were doing their jobs slowly and were frequently **6** .... with colds, back pain and headaches affected **7** .... , so that less was being produced per working day than ten years ago. The consultant recommended that Sophie should introduce a **8** .... , so that workers were paid extra for being more productive. Also, he suggested that a more flexible working system would help **9** .... and mean fewer people leaving the company.

2 Choose the best option – A, B or C – for each sentence.

1 Only 2% of our customers complain, so in comparison with our satisfied customers, they are a ....*B*.... .
   A limited number   B tiny minority   C significant number

2 The .... of banks – 95%, in fact – increased their profits last year.
   A vast majority   B growing numbers   C significant number

3 Internet use is becoming increasingly popular amongst older people and .... of them are shopping online.
   A a smaller percentage   B a limited number   C growing numbers

4 At the Annual General Meeting, Magdi Assad was elected with a .... of the votes – nearly 65%.
   A growing number   B substantial majority   C vast majority

5 A .... of people, perhaps as much as 35%, said they would be interested in buying our product.
   A significant number   B limited number   C growing number

Grammar

1 **Read these sentences, which are in reported speech, then write the original words which the speaker used in your notebook.**

1 He told me he was going to book his flight online.
  'I'm going to book my flight online.'
2 She said she worked for a bank in New York.
3 Marcelle told Sheila she had never worked in accounts before.
4 Danielle said she had already printed out the sales forecast.
5 Leo said he would fix the meeting for three o'clock the next day.
6 Maxine said she couldn't speak to me because she was busy.
7 Caroline told me they might change the computer system the following year.
8 Kamal said they had bought new software the previous month.
9 He said that the sales figures were bad.

2 **In your notebook, put these sentences into reported speech using the reporting verb given in brackets.**

1 'Oil prices are going to fall,' said the minister. (*predicted*)
  The minister predicted that oil prices were going to fall.
2 'Go to Berlin on the next plane,' said my boss. (*ordered*)
3 'There has been a 3% drop in market share,' I told them. (*informed*)
4 'Would you mind phoning the suppliers?' she said to Helga. (*requested*)
5 'When can you deliver the goods?' I asked her. (*enquired*)
6 'I'll have that report on your desk by midday tomorrow,' I told my boss. (*promised*)
7 'We don't know how much the development costs will be,' said the project leader. (*answered*)

3 **Each of these sentences has one mistake. Rewrite them correctly in your notebook.**

1 He said me he would give me a discount.
  He told me he would give me a discount. / He said he would give me a discount.
2 He told to me that the package had been sent the day before.
3 She explained him that she would prefer flexible working to part-time working.
4 He answered that he had changed jobs the last year.
5 She asked him how much did the flights cost.
6 He promised me that he will send the goods last week.
7 The caller enquired when would the product be launched.
8 He explained that he has forgotten to send the invoice.
9 He ordered her that she signed the cheque for $10,000.
10 I told him to not send the application by email.

Vocabulary

Match these words/phrases (1–8) (from the reading text on pages 92–93 of the Student's Book) with their definitions below (a–h) taken from the *Cambridge Business Dictionary* (CBD).

1 return

2 financial gains

3 payroll taxes

4 benefits

5 overhead costs

6 base salary

7 cashflow projection

8 cost savings

a advantages such as medical insurance, life insurance and sick pay that employees receive from their employer in addition to money

b amount of money that is saved or not spent

c amount paid to the government based on employees' pay, and is either paid by an employer or partly taken by an employer from what employees earn

d increase in money / extra money you make

e plan of how much money a company expects to spend and receive over a particular period

f the amount of money that someone earns every year in their job, not including any extra payments they may receive

g the amount of profit made by an investment or a business activity

h the cost of something that is not directly involved in making a particular product or providing a particular service, for example the cost of renting a building or of training staff

Grammar

1 Complete these sentences by writing the correct form of the verbs in brackets in the gaps.

1 If the company _hadn't run_ (not run) into financial trouble last year, we .... (not make) 300 staff redundant.

2 If the Board .... (not decide) to outsource our IT, it .... (be) difficult to reduce our overheads last year.

3 We .... (achieve) considerable cost savings if we had outsourced the office cleaning.

4 Our financial gains .... (be) much greater if the government .... (cut) payroll taxes in the last budget.

5 If their financial controller .... (make) a more accurate cashflow projection, we .... (make) a profit in the last quarter.

2 **Complete these sentences in any way you wish in your notebook.**
1 If I hadn't studied .... at college, I …
   If I hadn't studied accountancy at college, I wouldn't have got this job at Accenture.
2 If I could have studied something different, I …
3 I wouldn't have applied for a job at .... if …
4 If I could have got a job in a different country, I …
5 I wouldn't have got my first job unless …

Reading

You work for an import agency in your country. Read this letter from a UK
company. In most lines, there is one extra word. However, some lines are
correct. Cross out the extra word. If the line is correct, put a tick (✓).

Dear Sir or Madam,	
We are a producer of top-quality frozen fish and vegetables ~~being~~ based	1
in Felixstowe, England. Our customers do consist of large retail chains	2
and are leading supermarkets throughout the United Kingdom.	3
At present time, we are investigating the possibility of expanding our	4
export market and we are wondering what potential your country has	5
made for our products. We would be interested in selling to supermarkets	6
and could offer a very competitive prices. You will find enclosed a brochure	7
is giving details of our products.	8
I would be grateful if you could to tell us:	9
1 if do you think there is a market for our products in your country	10
2 whether you would be interested in acting as an import agent and	11
distributor on our behalf.	12
I am also considering visiting to your country next March in order to do	13
some fact-finding. During my visit, I would be welcome an opportunity	14
to meet you. Can you suggest giving some suitable dates in March	15
month for a visit?	16
I look forward to hearing from you.	
Yours faithfully,	
Jonathan Barraclough	
Export Manager	

Writing

Write a letter answering the letter above.
• Say that you are interested.
• Explain there is a market.
• Suggest dates for a meeting.

21 Customer satisfaction and loyalty

Vocabulary

Read this text. For each gap, choose the best word – A, B, C or D.

As every manager knows, 'the customer comes **1** _B_' and 'the customer is always right'. Despite these phrases being repeated so often, it is remarkable how many organisations **2** .... essential training in customer care. All too frequently when **3** .... front-office staff, customers are met with rudeness, lack of interest or **4** .... of stress, and these all give a negative **5** .... of the organisation itself. Many customers have come to **6** .... treatment of this kind, and as a **7** .... behave aggressively or irritably themselves. These customers very often are the 'awkward customers' whom even well-trained customer-service staff find hard to **8** .... Many experts believe that not **9** .... in an organisation has the right personality for a customer-service position and that this should be taken into **10** .... when recruiting front-line staff. Even with training, some people will never have the people **11** .... to deal successfully with customers in what can be a very stressful **12** .... There are also a number of experts who advocate training for customers in how to **13** .... the best out of the staff they have to deal with. However, this would only really be **14** .... in company-to-company situations where, for instance, company buyers have to deal with people from a **15** .... of different suppliers.

	A	B	C	D
1	top	first	best	ahead
2	abandon	stop	neglect	drop
3	approaching	reaching	arriving	talking
4	signals	shows	signs	appearances
5	view	opinion	idea	impression
6	expect	wait	hope	worry
7	result	feedback	principle	summary
8	deal	treat	look	handle
9	anyone	someone	no one	everyone
10	thought	account	granted	advantage
11	skills	knowledge	abilities	capabilities
12	location	work	appointment	post
13	obtain	take	extract	get
14	able	capable	practical	competent
15	quantity	number	amount	selection

(1 B is circled)

Grammar

1 **Write the correct relative pronoun in each gap in this email. Leave the gap blank if no pronoun is necessary.**

Hello, Sam

Do you remember the customer **1** ...*who*... called from Odessa last month? Well, she has just called again to complain that the tool **2** .... we sent her was not the one **3** .... she ordered. She says that **4** .... she wanted was the OH200, not the OH300. Andrew wants to know who is responsible for this. You are the one **5** .... handwriting is on the order form, and in the space **6** .... you have to write the product type, you have written OH200, but very indistinctly, and that could be the reason **7** .... the order was mixed up.

8 .... you need to do is:

• explain to Andrew, **9** .... is pretty angry, I warn you

• sort the thing out with the customer in Odessa – I suggest you send a replacement tool by those express couriers **10** .... number is on the notice board.

Thanks
Mary

---

2 **Join these sentences by using relative clauses.**

1 There's a man on the phone. He says he spoke to you yesterday.
   There's a man on the phone who says he spoke to you yesterday.

2 Did you repair the computer? It wasn't working.

3 I phoned the customer. His invoice hadn't arrived.

4 We stayed at an excellent hotel. It was near the city centre.

5 I work for a software company. Its headquarters are in Silicon Valley.

6 Have you visited the factory? They make the components there.

7 Claudio is the technician. He knows how to install the equipment.

8 We'll hold the meeting at 11 o'clock. Everyone is free then.

9 You forgot to answer the letter. I wrote it.

22 Communication with customers

Vocabulary

Choose the adjective in *italics* which collocates with the noun in each of these sentences.

1 China is a (big)/ *great* customer for our products.
2 Due to his excellent presentation skills, he has a *high* / *good* reputation throughout Russia.
3 The company manufactures a *wide* / *big* range of industrial cleaning products which they sell in *big* / *huge* quantities.
4 There have been *important* / *serious* problems on the production line today, and we've been making a(n) *important* / *tremendous* effort to solve them.
5 What a *big* / *large* number of people at the trade fair this year!

Grammar

Complete each of these sentences with a preposition.

1 Her company has a commitment ......*to*...... giving good service.

2 If you're dissatisfied .... the service, you ought to complain.

3 Few customers ever complain .... the price of our products.

4 She tries to build long-term relationships .... her clients.

5 One of his duties is to take care .... customer relationships.

6 I'm responsible .... updating the company website.

7 Our employees show tremendous loyalty .... the company.

8 What methods do you have for communicating .... your customers?

9 The best way .... keeping your customers is by exceeding their expectations.

10 We have been successfully competing .... two much larger companies for more than ten years.

11 You should focus .... the clients who spend the most money.

12 His irresponsible behaviour resulted .... a commercial disaster.

Writing

1 Study this chart and the handwritten notes. Then complete the sales report below by writing one word from the phrases expressing causes which you have studied in each gap.

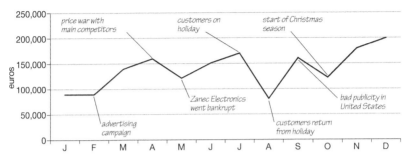

Sales – Benton Electronics

Report on sales: Benton Electronics

Our sales from January to February stayed the same at €90,000. However, in March, 1 ....*due*.... to our advertising campaign, sales increased by €50,000 to reach a level of €140,000. This trend continued in April, with sales of €160,000. Unfortunately, between April and May, we had a price war with our competitors, and this 2 .... in a fall in sales of €40,000. However, during May, our competitor, Zanec Electronics, went bankrupt, and this 3 .... to an increase over the next two months of €50,000.

At the end of July, most of our customers went on holiday, and this 4 .... a fall in sales of €90,000. However, when they returned in August, sales recovered, reaching a level of €160,000 in September. As a 5 .... of bad publicity in the US in September, our sales for October dropped to €120,000, but 6 .... to the Christmas season, they recovered to reach €200,000 in December.

2 Write a sales report for Carmel Sun Creams. Use the information on this chart and the handwritten notes. Use the report in Exercise 1 as a model.

Sales – Carmel Sun Creams

Vocabulary

1 **Complete each of these sentences by writing *last* or *latest* in the gaps.**

1 Have you heard the _latest_ news about Prussia Airlines? Their share price has risen sharply.

2 In the .... company I worked for, we paid much more attention to customers' opinions.

3 This is the .... time I'm going to this conference – it's such a waste of time!

4 Before we went into the meeting, we were all give the .... tablet PC to follow the Chairman's presentation on.

2 a **Match the verbs (1–8) with the noun or noun phrases (a–h) to form collocations. For two verbs, more than one collocation is possible.**

1 charge   a   a face-to-face meeting
2 extend   b   construction work
3 do   c   costs
4 carry out   d   high prices
5 organise   e   our range of services
6 meet   f   your requirements
7 calculate   g   trouble-free business
8 organise   h   work schedules

b **Complete each of these sentences with a collocation from Exercise 2a.**

1 Although they _charge high prices_, there is no doubt that their services offer value for money.

2 I hope the services we offer will .... and that we will be able to add you to our long list of satisfied customers.

3 I'm fed up with discussing all these things over the phone. I think we should .... as soon as possible.

4 Our excellent range of video-conferencing equipment will help you to .... from anywhere in your building.

5 The building company is arriving tomorrow to .... on the other side of the staff car park.

6 The work is very complex, so it's very hard to .... exactly. However, we will try to produce the most competitive estimate we can.

7 We have decided to .... by including accounting and auditing among the things we do.

8 With so many new projects starting, it's difficult to .... so that everyone is occupied and no one has too much work to do.

3 **Complete these sentences with the correct form of the words in brackets.**

1 We prefer to concentrate our efforts on *existing* customers rather than look for new ones. (*exist*)

2 Bad publicity from .... customers can be very damaging to a firm. (*satisfy*)

3 Please allow seven days from placing the order to date of .... (*deliver*)

4 The report is ...., so don't leave it lying around on your desk – lock it in a drawer. (*confident*)

5 Mallory's service is pretty .... – you never know when they're going to deliver the goods. (*rely*)

6 Doing this job by hand is so .... compared with doing it by machine. It wastes a lot of time. (*efficient*)

7 He has an .... network of contacts who can help him whenever he has a problem. (*extend*)

8 Our products give .... results, so I'm sure you'll be one of our many satisfied customers. (*guarantee*)

9 As a .... long-standing customer, we would like you to take advantage of this special offer. (*value*)

Grammar

In your notebook, express the following causes and results using the words given in brackets.

1 Our printer ran out of ink, and we had to address all the letters by hand. (*meant*)

Our printer ran out of ink, and this meant us having to address all the letters by hand.

OR *Our printer ran out of ink, and this meant that we had to address all the letters by hand.*

2 Unfortunately, Central Europe was hit by heavy storms last week, and we have fallen behind with our deliveries. (*consequence*)

3 There was a power cut in our area last week. Our computer system was down. (*meant*)

4 Our suppliers were late sending us some components. We were unable to complete your order on time. (*result*)

5 I am pleased to inform you that our suppliers have given us a considerable discount. We are in a position to offer you the goods you have ordered at a reduced price. (*consequently*)

6 Unfortunately, my secretary copied your telephone number incorrectly. I was unable to contact you. (*meant*)

24 Business across cultures

Vocabulary

1 **Choose the best word – A, B, C or D – for each gap.**

1 The successful candidate for this post will probably be ....*D*........externally.
   A contracted   B engaged   C taken on   ⟨D recruited⟩

2 We will have to work through the weekend in order to meet the ....
   we've been set.
   A bottom line   B last time   C deadline   D final hour

3 You should inform your superior as soon as possible if you think you are
   going to have difficulty in .... targets.
   A meeting   B finding   C arriving   D getting

4 We have sent free .... of the product to all our most important
   customers.
   A samples   B examples   C instances   D shows

5 The recent advertising .... was designed to boost brand awareness.
   A battle   B war   C fight   D campaign

6 Customer service is what gives the company a(n) .... over the
   competition.
   A edge   B side   C line   D border

7 It's important to keep .... to a minimum if you are going to make a
   decent profit.
   A oversights   B overheads   C overalls   D overwork

8 We expect retailers to add a 100% .... on our products when they sell
   them.
   A margin   B extra   C addition   D mark-up

9 When he needed to raise a loan, he used his .... , including his
   house, as security.
   A assets   B liabilities   C turnover   D fixtures

10 The interest .... has been raised to 5% this week.
   A rate   B type   C cost   D percentage

11 Entrepreneurs are people who enjoy .... risks.
   A making   B having   C taking   D doing

12 Doing the VAT returns is a very time-............... task.
   A using   B consuming   C spending   D wasting

13 Our respondents .... quality of service as the most important thing in
   the survey.
   A evaluated   B assessed   C appraised   D rated

14 Poor quality control is unlikely to .... the company's image.
   A enhance   B better   C grow   D reform

15 This year, our debts have .... to less than 10% of turnover.
   A lowered   B reduced   C cut   D decreased

2 Complete the presentation below by writing the word/phrase from the box that the speaker uses to structure the talk in each gap.

> because that way Finally Firstly However I think there are three things
> If you bear those things in mind Secondly To take a personal example You see

1 *I think there are three things* which are essential when taking up employment abroad. **2** .... , you have to be culturally sensitive. It's no good thinking that you are going to behave in exactly the same way at work as you did in your home country, **3** .... you'll just irritate people and you won't work so effectively. **4** .... , I come from Russia where bosses and managers tend to make decisions and staff have to accept them. **5** .... , if you're a manager, it's no use being autocratic in the United States, where there's a culture of discussing and consulting before making decisions. **6** .... , it's worth learning the language well, both written and spoken. If you don't, you'll have problems doing your job, however skilled you are. **7** .... , people will misunderstand you and they'll get impatient with you. **8** .... , there's no point in telling people how you do things in your country all the time. You have to fit into their context and understand things from their point of view. **9** .... , you'll have much less difficulty in achieving success.

Grammar

1 Complete each of these sentences by writing one word in each gap.

1 You'll have *difficulty* fitting into the workplace if you don't adopt local customs.
2 We're .... serious problems sourcing components for our new machines.
3 There's no .... in arguing with her – her mind is made up.
4 It's just not .... writing that email if no one is going to read it.
5 It is .... good cutting the budget if it's going to lead to lower revenues.
6 .... is no use insisting on staff arriving on time when the trains are on strike.

2 Finish these sentences in any way you like.
1 When you're looking for a job, it's worth …
2 When you're travelling for work to meet clients, it's no good …
3 In business meetings, it's really no use …
4 When speaking English in business situations, I always have problems …
5 When it comes to new office equipment, there's no point in …
6 In the company where I work, you won't have any difficulties …

Writing supplement

Punctuation and spelling

Punctuation

1 Match each number in this email with a rule on the use of commas (a–i) below. One rule refers to two numbers.

Example: 1 *d*

To: Ahmed Aziz
Subject: Visit to Seville

Dear Mr Aziz,[1]

Thank you for your enquiry about our wind-turbine components,[2] which you saw at the Spanish Wind Exhibition last month. I am pleased to attach our brochure with our complete range. You will see the brochure is in English and Spanish,[3] but not, unfortunately, in Arabic.

When we met at the Exhibition,[4] you also mentioned the possibility of visiting our offices in Seville in order to discuss a possible order. Would either the 17th,[5] 18th or 19th suit you? If none of these dates is convenient,[6] we could perhaps manage the following week. I would not be able to attend a meeting that week because I will be on annual leave. However,[7] my colleagues Felipe Barras,[8] Monica Herras[9] and Juan Ventoso would be happy to help you.

Looking forward to your early reply.

Yours sincerely,[10]

Gonzalo Punzal

Marketing Manager

Use a comma:

a after a conditional clause at the beginning of a sentence.

b after a time clause or other subordinate clause when they begin a sentence.

c after adverbs like *however, in spite of this, unfortunately, frankly,* etc. when they begin a sentence.

d after the person's name at the beginning of the letter.

e after *Yours sincerely* or *Yours faithfully* at the end of a letter or formal email.

f before and after a non-defining relative clause (see Student's Book page 114).

g before *but.*

h to separate things on a list.

Do not use a comma:

i before *and.*

2 **Find examples of these rules (a–f) on when to use capital letters in the email in Exercise 1.**

Use a capital letter…
a at the beginning of sentences. *You will see …*
b with names of events, books or places.
c with names of languages.
d with nationalities.
e with someone's name and title (*Mr, Dr*, etc.)
f with people's job titles

3 **Insert capital letters and commas in this email where necessary.**

To:	Gonzalo Punzal
Subject:	Re: Visit to Seville

dear mr punzal *Dear …*
unfortunately I won't be able to meet you on the dates you mentioned as I already have a trip to austria booked for that week. however if you are free the first week in may would be a very convenient time for me to come and see how the spanish manufacture components.
when I was last in seville about three years ago I stayed at the hotel inglaterra which is right in the city centre. would that be the best hotel to stay at on this occasion or can you recommend somewhere else? also I hope to visit you with three or four colleagues if that is ok because we hope to place quite a large order. as we will need to look at the figures quite closely one of the team will be the chief accountant mr felahi. the operations manager the production manager and his assistant will also be coming.
please let me know if the suggested dates are convenient for you.
yours sincerely
ahmed aziz
chief executive

4 **This email contains 12 mistakes in punctuation (but not just commas and capital letters). Find and correct them.**

1 *Dear Mr Aziz,*

To:	Ahmed Aziz
Subject:	Re: Visit to Seville

Dear Mr Aziz
I am delighted you are able to come with your team who I am keen to meet. The Hotel Inglaterra is a good hotel. However we have taken the liberty of reserving rooms for you all at the hotel Alfonso XIII which is very near to our offices. As you are our prospective customers and guests in our city we would be happy to pay all your expenses during your stay Therefore could you please let us know exactly when you will be arriving so we can send a limousine to collect you your accountant, and your other colleagues from the airport, which is about 30 minutes from the city?
I look forward to hearing from you and meeting you again.
Yours Sincerely
Gonzalo Punzal
Marketing Manager

Spelling

1 ⊘ There are some words which Business English students often spell wrong. Look at this list of words and underline the word in the column – A or B – which is spelled correctly.

	A	B
1	<u>accommodation</u>	accomodation
2	advertisment	advertisement
3	which	wich
4	oportunity	opportunity
5	convenient	convinient
6	greatful	grateful
7	believe	belive
8	course	cours
9	enviroment	environment
10	neccessary	necessary
11	Madam	Madame
12	experence	experience
13	begining	beginning
14	communicate	comunicate
15	because	becaus
16	excelent	excellent
17	forward	foward
18	prefer	preffer
19	recived	received
20	recommend	reccommend
21	ofice	office
22	bussiness	business

2 Read this email and correct the 12 spelling mistakes.

> **To:**   Astrid Henkel
> **Subject:** Product launch Vienna
>
> Dear Astrid,
>   planning
> We're ~~planing~~ to come to Vienna on 13th February for three days for the product launch and are looking for accommodation near the city centre. I would be greatful if you could recomend somewhere suitable for us to stay, if posible near your offices. My team has expressed a preferrence for somewhere in the old town. While we're in Vienna, it would be excelent if we could have the oportunity to meet you and discuss our respective businesses, as we believe we have a lot in common and have some ideas for joint venture. Can you sugest a time wich would be convenient for you, preferably towards the begining of our stay? Many thanks and looking froward to seeing you again.
> Kind regards,
> Piotr

3 ⊙ Business English students often make spelling mistakes when adding *-ed* and *-ing* to verbs. Complete the gaps in each of these rules (1–7) for adding *-ed* and *-ing* to verbs with one of the examples below (a–g).

Spelling changes when adding *-ed* and *-ing* to verbs

We double the final consonant* when we add *-ed* or *-ing* to:
- a one-syllable verb which ends in a consonant–vowel*–consonant: ..f.. 1
- verbs of two or more syllables which end in consonant–vowel–consonant and the final syllable is stressed: 2

We don't double the final consonant when:
- there are two final consonants: 3
- there are two vowels before the final consonant: 4
- the stress is not on the final syllable in words of two or more syllables: 5
- the verb ends in *w, x* or *y*: 6**

When adding *-ed*, a final *y* after a consonant becomes *i*: 7

* Consonants are *b, c, d, f, g,* etc. Vowels are *a, e, i, o* and *u*.

** Note: *pay* is irregular – the past is *paid*.

---

a	*open* → *opened*	**e**	*fund* → *funded*
b	*begin* → *beginning*	**f**	~~*stop*~~ → ~~*stopped*~~
c	*meet* → *meeting*	**g**	*study* → *studied*
d	*pay* → *paying*		

4 Complete this email by adding *-ing* or *-ed* to the verbs in brackets and making any necessary spelling changes.

To: Melanie Leblanc
Subject: Computer crash
Hi Melanie,
I'm **1** writing (*write*) to apologise to you about the problem which **2** .... (*occur*) with the computers this morning. I **3** .... (*try*) **4** .... (*phone*) you earlier, but was **5** .... (*inform*) you were **6** .... (*speak*) to clients.
As I **7** .... (*mention*) last week, we've been **8** .... (*run*) some new programs on the computers, and as a result, some of them have been **9** .... (*crash*). These are programs which have been **10** .... (*develop*) by our in-house team and are just **11** .... (*come*) to the stage where we can roll them out. We are **12** .... (*hope*) and **13** .... (*plan*) to use them throughout the company sometime soon.
There are bound to be some glitches when we're **14** .... (*start*) out, but we're **15** .... (*refer*) these back to the technical guys, who I'm sure will soon have them **16** .... (*iron*) out.
Sorry about all the inconvenience.
Regards,
Ashram

---

5 You are Melanie's assistant. She has left you this note. Write the email.

> Hi,
>
> Can you write a short reply to Ashram:
> * explaining why I can't reply myself
> * complaining about the disruption to office work
> * asking for a warning in future?
>
> Thanks, Mel

Organising your writing

Paragraphing

1 In order to write in a clear, well-organised way, you should write in paragraphs. Each paragraph should deal with a different aspect of the topic. Put the paragraphs in this email in the most logical order.

To: Lily Choy
Subject: New office in Shenzhen
Hello Lily,

☐ a | Initially, we would aim to have just a small office employing a maximum of three staff, consisting of a local manager and one or two locally recruited assistants, so we would probably need just two rooms, or perhaps three. These would be a front office for receiving visitors and to exhibit some samples of our products and a back office where staff would work. The office should be in a smart, modern building which reflects our company's image.

☐ b | I'm writing because I've been asked to investigate the possibility of our opening an office in Shenzhen, so that we can have local representation in that part of China. I thought my first step should be to ask your advice about how to find suitable premises and who to approach.

☐ c | Thanking you in advance, and I look forward to hearing from you.

☐ d | If you think you can help me with this, would you be able to accompany me on a trip to Shenzhen to look at possible premises, interpret where necessary with local property owners and generally advise me? If you can help me in this way, please let me know how soon you will be able to do this. We would, of course, pay you a fee for your services and all your expenses.

☑ e | I hope you're well.

☐ f | We hope to rent the office space in the first instance.

Teresa Krantz

2 **Note down the subject of each paragraph in the email in Exercise 1.**

Paragraph 1 – an informal greeting

3 **Read Lily's reply and divide it into paragraphs by writing // where one paragraph should end and another begin.**

To: Teresa Krantz
Subject: Re: New office in Shenzhen
Hi Teresa,
Good to hear from you, and I hope you're well too. // I can indeed help you to find suitable premises, as I have several reliable and trustworthy contacts in the city who will be able to introduce us to estate agents and property managers. I'm sure we'll be able to look at a number of buildings that match the requirements you've stated in your email, so you'll have plenty of choice. As I'm sure you realise, Shenzhen is a booming city, and as a result, property prices and rents are sky high. Could you let me know what sort of price you'd be willing to pay for the sort of premises you describe so I can let my contacts know and they can start looking for us? It would also be helpful to know if you're looking for fully furnished and equipped offices, or whether you'd prefer to equip the office yourself. This will also impact on the rent, but on the other hand make it much easier to get started. I'd be happy to accompany you to Shenzhen, and the first week in January would be a convenient time for me to do so. If that suits you as well, I'll set up meetings for that week. One last point: would you like me to assist you with recruiting local staff? If so, I'd be happy to contact local employment agencies on your behalf. However, you'll have to send me details of the posts you hope to recruit. I look forward to working with you on this project and I'll forward you details of possible premises when I hear back from my contacts.
Best wishes, Lily

---

4 **You have received this message from your boss. Write the email. Use Teresa's email in Exercise 1 as a model.**

To:
Subject: New premises – St Petersburg
Hi,
We've decided to open a representative office in St Petersburg – just a couple of people and an office. Can you write to Dimitri in Moscow and get him to help you find the right office? Tell him the sort of place we need and offer him a fee for his help.
Thanks,
Kurt

Linking paragraphs and ideas

1 a To help readers follow the logic of a piece of writing, you can add
      linking words and phrases at the beginning of a paragraph or sentence
      to link it to the paragraph or sentence which comes before. Complete
      the email below using the linking words and phrases in the box.

> As a result   However   The advantage of this is that   Unfortunately, though
> When customers visit the site   When they do this

To: Lindsay Macdonald
Subject: Website glitches
Dear Lindsay,
We've been experiencing a few problems with our website, and I'm writing to ask
if you can give us a hand in solving <u>them</u>[1]. I'll explain what's happening.
1 .... , <u>they</u>[2] have the option of ordering and paying for goods directly by
giving their credit-card details, address and so on. <u>This</u>[3] is working fine.
2 .... , they also have the alternative option of registering. **3** .... , they
give themselves a user name and a password. **4** .... we save their credit-
card details, and <u>this</u>[4] makes buying goods on repeat visits much easier.
5 .... , we're finding that when users log on, the website does not
automatically bring up their details. <u>This</u>[5] means <u>they</u>[6] have to go through the
process of filling in their details yet again. **6** .... , customers are finding that
repeat purchases are not quicker, and we risk losing them if <u>this</u>[7] is not fixed
quickly.
Can you help? <u>It</u>'s[8] quite urgent.
Kind regards,
Don

---

   b Read the email again with the linking words/phrases and notice how it
      is easier to follow.

2 What is the purpose of each paragraph in the email in Exercise 1a?

3 Writers use words within sentences to refer to other parts of their text.
   What does each of the underlined words in the email in Exercise 1a
   refer to?

4 A piece of equipment in your office is not working properly. Write an email
   to the technician:
   • saying which piece of equipment is not working properly
   • explaining the problem and what the results of the problem are
   • asking for his help and explaining why it is urgent.

   You can use the email in Exercise 1a as a model.

Planning letters and emails

1 **Success in communication is partly the result of planning and organisation. Look at this email from your boss and organise the plan below into the most logical order by choosing which point (a–f) you would put in each paragraph of your reply (1–4).**

To:
Subject: Website
Hi,
Our website needs completely modernising – it hasn't been done in five years. Can you write an email to each of the web developers listed below asking them for a sample design and to quote for the job?
Thanks,
Marisa

a ask for a quote
b ask for samples
c explain what work we need and why
d introduce our company
e offer to supply further information
f say where we heard about them

2 **Read this email. In which paragraph does the writer include each of the points (a–f) from Exercise 1?**

To: Undisclosed recipients
Subject: Quote for redesign of website
Dear Sir/Madam,
We are a small logistics company based in Clermont-Ferrand, France, specialising in the international transport of nuclear isotopes and other high-value, high-risk materials for hospitals throughout Europe.
At present, we are looking for a web developer to give our website an entirely new, modern appearance in keeping with the image we want to project. This is because our current website, which you can see at www.clerlogists.com, has not been significantly updated in several years, and our previous web developer is no longer in business. A particular requirement we have for the new website is that it must be attractive and easy to navigate. The information and links it contains would remain the same.
Your company has been recommended to us by our partners, Transvite in Poitiers, and we would be grateful if you could supply us with some sample designs to consider and choose from and an estimate of the cost of this work.
If you require any further information, please do not hesitate to contact me.
Many thanks, and I look forward to hearing from you.
Yours faithfully,

3 a The company where you work, or a company you know well, needs its brochure updating and redoing. Your manager has asked you to write to a graphic design company explaining what you need and asking for a sample design and a quote. Write a brief plan for the email.

   b Write the email following your plan. You can use the email in Exercise 2 as a model.

4 Look at this task and the extract from the management minutes below. Decide what you want to achieve by writing the letter.

> You work as Assistant Office Manager in a direct mail company. You have been asked to write a letter to Hans Spindler, the Sales Manager of QB Supplies, which sells your company its office supplies, to complain about its services.

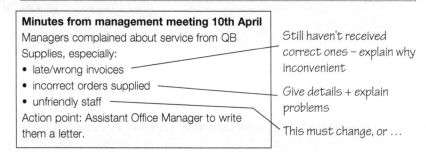

Minutes from management meeting 10th April
Managers complained about service from QB Supplies, especially:
• late/wrong invoices
• incorrect orders supplied
• unfriendly staff
Action point: Assistant Office Manager to write them a letter.

Still haven't received correct ones – explain why inconvenient

Give details + explain problems

This must change, or …

5 Look again at the management minutes in Exercise 4 on which you have made some handwritten notes. Write a plan for your letter.
   • Use all the handwritten notes.
   • Decide what the purpose of each paragraph is.
   • Decide what each paragraph should contain.

6 Write your letter following your plan.

7 Look at the sample letter on page 66 and do the exercises.

Linking ideas in short emails

1 Read this short email and underline the words/phrases the writer uses to link ideas

> **To:** Flora Marcovitz
> **Subject:** Fire practice
> Hi Flora,
> In order to comply with local fire regulations, we will be holding a fire practice in the building sometime next week. We are not giving the exact time for this, because we want people to treat it as if it was a real emergency. With this in mind, could you check that all fire exits are working properly?
> Many thanks,
> Birgit

2 **Answer these questions about the email in Exercise 1.**

1 What request does Birgit make?
2 What reason does she give for her request?
3 What reason does she give for:
   a holding a fire practice?
   b not specifying when it will happen?

3 **Complete the email below by writing a linking word/phrase from the box in each gap. You will not need all of the words/phrases.**

| however   in order to   this   this meant   unless   which   with the purpose of |

To: Tanya Stankova
Subject: Health and safety inspection
Dear Tanya,
1 .... prepare for the health and safety inspection next month, could you please make sure that all fire extinguishers have been serviced correctly? As you know, **2** .... wasn't the case last time and **3** .... , we received a large fine **4** .... we would like to avoid this time.
Thanks,
Maximilian

---

4 **Do these three writing tasks. Use linking words/phrases where necessary.**

1 You have heard that some important overseas clients will be visiting your company soon. Write an email to your line manager:
   • saying which clients will be visiting
   • explaining why their visit is important
   • suggesting how to entertain them.

2 Some equipment you bought for the office recently has not been delivered. Write an email to the supplier:
   • saying what the equipment is
   • asking why the equipment is late
   • explaining why you need it soon.

3 Your company has decided to send you to work for a year in one of its overseas offices. Write an email to your colleagues:
   • saying where you will be working
   • explaining why you will be working there
   • explaining what you will be doing in your new post.

5 **Look at the sample answers to the above tasks on pages 66–67 and do the exercises for each of them.**

6 **Compare your answers with the sample answers on pages 66–67.**
  - Did you cover all the same points?
  - Did you cover the points in the same order?
  - Which linking words/phrases in the sample answers could you use to improve your answers?

Planning reports and proposals

1 **Look at the task below and write a plan showing the:**
  - sections you think your report should contain
  - information/ideas you should put in each section.

Your company is planning changes in the way it recruits new graduates. Your line manager has asked you to write a report on the methods your company uses at present, recommending any changes you think should be made.

Write a report for your line manager on graduate recruitment in your company. In it, write about:
- how graduates are recruited at present
- how well the system works
- any problems with the system
- any changes you would recommend.

---

2 **Write your report following your plan. You can use the reports in the Student's Book Writing reference section on page 121 as models.**

3 **Compare your answer with the sample answer on page 67 and do the exercise which accompanies it.**

4 **Read this task and write a brief plan for your proposal.**

You are manager of a music store in your city. Your line manager at head office has asked you about opportunities to expand the business in your city.

Look at the information on the next page on which you have already made some handwritten notes.

Then write a brief plan for a **proposal**.

---

suggest this
because ...

two other music
stores nearby

say why this
location would
be good

easy to expand
here, but ...

We need to find ways of increasing market
share and revenue. Have you noticed any
ways we could expand in your city? Perhaps
expanding your present premises or a new
store in a different part of the city?

Empty stores available for rent

	rent per month
city centre	€12,000
opposite train station	€8,000
next to present store	€5,000

expensive,
but ...

5 Now write the proposal using your plan from Exercise 4. You can use the
proposals in the Student's Book Writing reference on page 122 as models.

6 Compare your answer with the sample answer on page 68 and do the
exercise which accompanies it.

7 Compare your answer with the sample answer on page 68. Check that:
  • your answer is divided into paragraphs
  • you used capital letters, full stops and commas correctly
  • you spelled your answer correctly (check your spelling by using a
    dictionary)
  • you used suitable linking words and phrases
  • you covered all the important points
  • the points are organised logically.

Sample answers

Planning letters and emails, Exercise 7

1 Read the sample letter below and answer these questions.

1 How does this letter compare with the letter you wrote?

2 What introductory and linking words/phrases could you use to fill the gaps?

2 Complete the letter with phrases from the box.

> Finally   For example   ~~I am writing to complain about~~   I would like to remind you that
> In addition to these problems   In another instance   The main problem has been that
> This has meant   with the result that

> Dear Mr Spindler,
> 1 .I.am.writing.to.complain.about........ the inadequate service we have been
> receiving from your company recently.
> 2 .... our orders have not been supplied correctly on a number of
> occasions. 3 .... , you omitted to supply toner for the printers and
> photocopier in our February order, 4 .... we were unable to print documents
> for two days. 5 .... , you supplied us with ordinary paper where we had
> ordered recycled paper.
> 6 .... , you have invoiced us for a number of items we never ordered, and
> your invoices arrived too late to be included in the correct accounting period.
> 7 .... extra work for the accounts staff sorting out the confusion.
> 8 .... , when our staff have phoned your staff to point out these deficiencies,
> they have on occasions been given impolite and unco-operative answers.
> 9 .... we have been regular customers of yours for a number of years and
> have always settled your invoices promptly. Unless we receive the friendly,
> efficient service we expect, we will order our office supplies from one of your
> competitors.
> Yours sincerely,

Linking ideas in short emails, Exercise 5

1 Complete this sample answer for Task 1 by writing one word in each gap.

> Dear Antonio
> The Purchasing Manager and the Production Manager from Slezak SA will
> be paying a visit to our offices next week in 1 .... to finalise details of
> the contract 2 .... has been negotiated. So 3 .... to make them feel
> welcome 4 .... they are here, I think we should invite them to dinner at the
> Curio restaurant in the evening.
> Best wishes

2 Organise the phrases listed below into the correct order for this sample answer to Task 2. Add any commas, full stops and capital letters you think are necessary.

> *Dear Mr Kreisky,*
> and they need the computers
> as we have just taken on new staff as part of our expansion
> I would be grateful if you could explain why   1
> in order to work efficiently
> it is essential that you deliver them immediately
> we still have not received the eight computers
> which we purchased from your store last week
> *Yours sincerely,*

3 Complete the sample answer below to Task 3 using the phrases in the box.

> in order to help   I'm happy to say   with the aim of   While I'm there

> Dear colleagues,
> **1** .... that I have been posted to our office in Nairobi for the next year
> **2** .... expand our East African operations. **3** .... , my main duty will be to identify new clients for our services **4** .... generating new business.
> Best wishes,

Planning reports and proposals, Exercise 3

Divide this sample report into sections and decide what heading each section should have.

> **Report on graduate recruitment at Bendex, SA**
> The purpose of this report is to summarise how we currently find and take on graduate trainees and to recommend changes to the system.
> At present, we recruit graduates by advertising vacancies through university careers services. Students complete an application form and need a recommendation from a teacher or tutor.
> We filter these applications and invite suitable applicants to a preliminary interview. Applicants who pass this interview then do a series of psychometric tests, along with further more demanding interviews before being selected.
> The system works reasonably well. About 45 applicants normally attend the preliminary interview. From these, we select 20 to go through the other parts of the process. Our average graduate intake is seven graduates a year, and their quality has been very satisfactory. However, each year two or three of these recruits tend to leave the company because they want more responsibility than we initially offer.
> I recommend that we give applicants clearer information about what their jobs will involve before they start. I would also suggest that we try to match the job possibilities more closely to our candidates' aspirations, as many of them are highly ambitious.

Planning reports and proposals, Exercise 6

Complete this sample answer by putting the sentences in the correct order and dividing it into paragraphs.

Proposal for expansion of Musicbug Stores in Mannheim

1   The aim of this proposal is to suggest an opportunity for expansion in Mannheim.
Also, two of our competitors already have shops in the area.

2   At present, we have one store located in the old city.
However, I would not recommend this, because we are meeting demand from our customers with no problems.
I favour this, because many young people go past this location every day.
I have found two possible locations.
In order to extend our market, I suggest that we should open new premises in another district of the city.
The first is in the city centre, but unfortunately the rent is rather high at €12,000 a month.
The second option is empty premises opposite the main railway station.
We could expand into the premises next to ours without difficulty.
What is more, it is less expensive than the city centre.

Answer key

Unit 1

Vocabulary
2 employees   3 degree   4 experience
5 development   6 training course
7 training   8 skills   9 qualifications
10 certificates

Grammar
1   2 C   3 C   4 C   5 C   6 C   7 U   8 C
    9 U   10 U   11 C   12 U   13 C
    14 C   15 U   16 U   17 C   18 C   19 U
    20 C   21 U   22 C   23 U   24 U
    25 U   26 U   27 C   28 C   29 U
    30 U   31 C   32 U   33 U   34 U
2   3 a   4 –   5 an   6 –   7 –   8 –
    9 a   10 –   11 –   12 a   13 a   14 –
3   2 How long   3 Which   4 Where
    5 How often   6 What   7 How many
    8 How much
4   2   Is there anything you dislike about
        your job? / Is there anything about
        your job you dislike?
    3   How often do you have to travel for
        your job?
    4   How many employees are there in
        your company?
    5   How did you get into this line of
        work?
    6   What do you think you will be doing
        in ten years' time?

Unit 2

Vocabulary
1   2 team leaders   3 projects   4 targets
    5 deadlines   6 launch   7 results
    8 budget
2   2 satisfied/satisfying/satisfactory
    3 development
    4 developing/developed/
      developmental
    5 supervisor/supervision
    6 supervisory
    7 manager/management
    8 managerial
    9 recruitment/recruiter/recruit
    10 challenge
    11 challenge/challenger
    12 responsibility
    13 performance
    14 investment

15 finance
16 financial
17 promoter/promotion
18 promoted
19 effect/efficacy
20 effective

Grammar
1   a   2 spent   3 moved
        4 have worked   5 have done
        6 was   7 has encouraged
        8 passed   9 became
2   2 worked/were working   3 decided
    4 had   5 has signed   6 has been
3   *Suggested answer*
    Two years ago, Pekov Steel recruited
    17 graduates. However, last year the
    number rose substantially to 48. This
    was because the company decided to
    expand into ship-building, which was
    a major new activity. This year, just 12
    graduates have been recruited because,
    as a result of the large intake last year
    and their training needs, fewer were
    needed.

Unit 3

Grammar
2 at/from   3 about   4 in/with
5 to   6 of   7 in   8 in   9 in
10 in/during/for   11 for/in/at
12 on/about   13 for/as   14 in
15 in   16 in

Reading
3 now   4 qualification   5 of
6 is   7 ✓   8 my   9 although   10 ✓
11 for   12 of   13 so   14 ✓   15 going
16 ✓   17 for   18 other   19 you   20 am

Vocabulary
1   2 pride   3 contribute   4 value
    5 lucky (happy)   6 interested
    7 rewarding   8 happy
2   2 detailed; informative   3 open
    4 convenient   5 interested   6 absent

Unit 4

Reading
2 to/with   3 Speaking   4 This
5 for   6 afraid   7 through   8 all

9 this/calling   10 This   11 afraid
12 take   13 possible   14 course
15 Thank

Grammar
1   3 most inconvenient   4 busiest
    5 more expensive / the most
    expensive   6 fewer   7 most/more
    8 less   9 more costly / costlier
    10 larger   11 more theoretical
    12 more hands-on
2   *Suggested answers*
    2 much less than   3 far sooner than
    4 much more difficult / much harder
    5 you must/should prepare
    6 slightly more formally than
    7 a lot less important than
    8 it really matters a lot

Unit 5

Vocabulary
1   2 A   3 C   4 A   5 D   6 D   7 B
    8 C   9 A   10 B   11 C   12 D
    13 C   14 B   15 D
2   2 d   3 f   4 b   5 g   6 e   7 a   8 h

Grammar
2 to be   3 increasing   4 to spend
5 to raise   6 losing   7 doing
8 following   9 contacting   10 to find out
11 doing   12 thinking   13 developing
14 innovating   15 to meet
16 to discuss   17 to see   18 hearing

Writing
Sample answer
Dear Vince
I think it would be a good idea to have a
meeting to discuss this, although I think
we'll find increasing the marketing budget
problematic because it's already very high
in relation to our other expenditure. How
about eleven o'clock on Tuesday?
Colin

Unit 6

Vocabulary
1   2 entrepreneurial
    3 skilful (UK) / skillful (US)
    4 commuter/commuting
    5 launch/launching
    6 establishment
    7 established
    8 option

9   optional
10 reliance
11 reliable
12 distribution/distributor
2   2 B   3 C   4 A   5 C   6 C   7 B   8 C
    9 A

Grammar and writing
1   1 by; to
    2 on; from; to
    3 on; of; from/on
2   *Sample answer*
The purpose of this report is to
summarise our promotional spending
on Turbobuzz last year and this year.
Our spending on advertising went up
by €50,000 to €550,000 as a result of
increased advertising charges in the
principal sports magazines. We also
sponsor an amateur football tournament
and we cut spending in this area from
€230,000 last year to €180,000 this year
because we felt we could achieve the
same results with a lower budget.
On the other hand, we have
substantially increased our spending on
free samples at athletics championships
from €170,000 last year to €350,000 this
year, as this is an Olympic year.
Our projected budget for next year is
€850,000, a reduction of €200,000 from
this year, but I suggest we increase
it slightly so that we can afford more
magazine advertising.

Unit 7

Vocabulary
1   *Suggested answers*
    customer base
    floor space
    furniture exhibition, furniture markets,
    furniture stand
    event organisers
    exhibition centre, exhibition material,
    exhibition organisers, exhibition space,
    exhibition stand
    export markets
    publicity material, publicity stand
2   2 exhibition centre
    3 exhibition stand
    4 export markets
    5 floor space
    6 customer base
    7 publicity material

Writing

1 2 in 3 of 4 who/which/that
5 our 6 if/whether 7 will/shall
8 Can/Could 9 that/which
10 forward

2 *Sample answer*
Dear Ms Skuja,
We would certainly be interested in discussing the possibility of acting as your agents. Our Managing Director, Pam Maguire, would be happy to meet you while you are here in New Zealand. Can we suggest that you visit our offices on 7 October at 10.30 a.m. if that is convenient?
Yours sincerely,

Reading

2 my 3 a 4 then 5 is 6 not 7 also
8 to

Grammar

1 tell; costs 2 would; if 3 grateful; could/would 4 if/whether; know
5 you; how

Unit 8

Vocabulary

1 2 B 3 A 4 B 5 B 6 A 7 A 8 A
2 2 profit margin 3 bulk orders
4 discount 5 reductions 6 mark-up
7 recommended retail price

Grammar

2 won't be 3 'd/would place
4 guaranteed; 'd/would allow
5 won't manage 6 arrive; 'll/will be
7 would/'d offer; were

Reading

2 to (2nd) 3 will 4 to (2nd)
5 However 6 back 7 be

Writing

Sample answer
Dear Marta,
Please see the email attached. I've checked our records, and everything seems correct, so they must have made a mistake at the bank. Could you phone them to find out what has caused this problem? Also, please call Ms Meyer to apologise and to tell her what has happened.
Thanks

Unit 9

Vocabulary

1 2 a 3 h 4 g 5 e 6 d 7 b 8 f 9 i
2 **a** 1 franchiser 2 franchisee
  b 1 employer, employee
    2 interviewer, interviewee
    3 trainer, trainee
    4 payer, payee
3 2 assets 3 liabilities 4 profits
  5 costs 6 rate 7 tax
4 2 do 3 making 4 go 5 doing
  6 go 7 going

Grammar

2 at 3 to/until/till 4 to 5 for 6 in
7 by 8 at 9 for 10 during
11 since 12 for

Writing

Sample answer
May,
As you know, Mr Chu is visiting us tomorrow. Could you please arrange for a taxi to pick him up from the station at 10.30 and also arrange a meeting room here from 10.40 till lunchtime? Also, I'd be grateful if you'd reserve a table at Antoine's for one o'clock.
Many thanks

Unit 10

Vocabulary

1 2 B 3 C 4 A 5 A 6 B 7 C
  8 D 9 C 10 A 11 D 12 B
  13 C 14 A
2 1 assets; collateral; loan
  2 market rate; tax returns
  3 market research; overheads; cashflow
  4 business plan; investors
  5 borrow

Writing

1 2 which 3 up 4 to 5 you/some
  6 an 7 on 8 let 9 not
  10 one/date/time/day
2 *Sample answer*
Dear Ms Hall,
Thank you for your letter applying to do work experience with our company. We would like to invite you to an interview where we can discuss your application at 11 a.m. on Tuesday 12 July at the above address.

Please telephone me to confirm that the date and time are convenient. We look forward to meeting you.

Yours sincerely,

Unit 11

Vocabulary

1 1 CEO: The others are all secretarial/administrative jobs.
   2 branch: The others are where the management is based.
   3 showroom: The others are where goods are stored.
   4 boardroom: The others are where goods are made.
   5 facility: The others are where goods are sold.
   6 shareholders: The others are people who manage the business.
   7 back office: The others are where development and research takes place.
   8 modify: The others relate to new products.

2 a *Suggested answers*
   cold calling
   cost cutting
   eye catching
   ground breaking
   job sharing
   knowledge sharing, knowledge building
   problem solving, problem sharing
   record breaking
   team building
   time consuming

   b 2 job-sharing   3 time consuming
   4 ground-breaking
   5 knowledge sharing
   6 team-building   7 cost cutting
   8 problem-solving
   9 record-breaking   10 eye-catching
   (Note: when used as adjectives before a noun, these compounds have a hyphen (-).)

Reading

2 ~~plot~~ plan   3 ~~In~~ At
4 ~~Although~~ However
5 ~~who~~ which/that   6 ~~to~~ for
7 ~~should~~ would   8 ~~become~~ be
9 ~~which~~ what   10 ~~shops~~ outlets
11 ~~suggested~~ suggest   12 ~~do~~ make
13 ~~band~~ team/department

14 ~~time~~ order   15 ~~this~~ these
16 ~~put~~ launch   17 ~~the~~ a   18 ~~in~~ for

Grammar

2 Although they had a large budget, they ran short of money.
3 In spite of carrying out market research, our product failed.
4 The company was extremely successful, although it had cashflow problems.
   OR Although the company was extremely successful, it had cashflow problems.
5 We decided to rent the premises, despite them/their being extremely expensive.
6 Our agent didn't understand the market, although he was a local man.
   OR Although our agent was a local man, he didn't understand the market.
7 In spite of us/our spending over £1m on advertising, brand awareness didn't improve.

Unit 12

Vocabulary

1 2 laptop   3 screen
   4 product samples   5 remote control
   6 pointer   7 data projector   8 flipchart
2 2 c   3 e   4 a   5 h   6 b   7 f   8 g   9 d

Grammar

1 2 have travelled   3 to hear
   4 have all had   5 introduce
   6 to explain   7 investing
   8 aim / am aiming
   9 shall/will give
   10 shall/will tell
   11 have been conducting / have conducted / are conducting
   12 shall/will outline   13 represents
   14 would like
   15 would/will/shall be   16 to answer
2 2 can   3 could   4 can/could   5 can
   6 could   7 can

Unit 13

Vocabulary and writing

1 2 B   3 C   4 C   5 B   6 C   7 D
   8 A   9 D   10 C   11 B   12 C
   13 B   14 B   15 D

2 *Sample answer*
Dear Sirs,
I'd like to book five double rooms for myself and my colleagues for the nights of 13th–15th July. If possible, could you please ensure that all rooms have views of the river?
Also, could you let me know if breakfast is included in the price?
We are planning to meet clients from companies in the Wroclaw area and will be needing a meeting room for the 13th and a conference room all day on the 14th. Would you please reserve these for us and let me know how much they will cost?
Thanking you in advance,

Grammar

1 2 should have cleaned
3 should have allowed
4 should have given
5 shouldn't / should not have had

2 *Suggested answers*
1 should have sent someone from the office to meet me.
2 should have been open 24 hours a day.
3 should have been more polite.
4 should have brought the luggage earlier / should have unloaded the plane more quickly / shouldn't have taken so long to unload the luggage.

Unit 14

Vocabulary

1 2 h   3 i   4 f   5 d   6 b   7 c   8 j
9 e   10 a

2 2 find out   3 note down   4 cut off
5 move on   6 fix up   7 pick; up
8 clear up / deal with
9 followed; up
10 deals with / follows up

3 2 unpersuasive   3 unproven
4 demotivating   5 unreliable
6 disorganised   7 uncommunicative

4 3 implementation
4 consultation/consultant/ consultancy
5 consultative
6 exhibition/exhibitor
7 presentation/presenter
8 operation/operator
9 operational

10 proof
11 proven
12 combination
13 combined
14 finance/financier
15 financial
16 motivation/motivator/motive
17 motivated/motivating/motivational
18 reliance/reliability
19 reliable
20 organisation/organiser
21 organised/organisational
22 communication/communicator
23 communicative

5 2 unreliable   3 uncommunicative
4 organised   5 proven   6 demotivating

Unit 15

Vocabulary

1 2 chair(person)   3 agenda
4 circulate   5 minutes   6 action

2 a 2 b   3 d   4 c   5 a
b 2 information sharing
3 team building
4 decision-making
5 problem-solving

3 Across: 3 call off   4 chair
6 adjourn   7 attend
Down: 2 put off   3 circulate   5 hold

Grammar
2 it   3 one   4 it   5 the others   6 This
7 them

Unit 16

Vocabulary

1 2 A   3 B   4 A   5 A   6 D   7 D
8 A   9 A   10 C   11 B   12 C
13 B   14 C   15 A

2 2 D   3 D   4 D   5 I   6 D   7 I   8 I
9 D   10 I   11 I   12 I

3 *Suggested answers*
2 recovered   3 going down   4 rose
5 plummeting   6 soared   7 fell
8 went up

Grammar
2 was launched   3 was adopted
4 have been produced
5 has recently been introduced
6 are expected   7 to be used
8 is hoped   9 will be opened
10 will be manufactured / will have been manufactured

Unit 17

Vocabulary
Suggested answers
2 getting/keeping 3 made 4 make
5 done / carried out 6 attended
7 meeting 8 implement 9 placed
10 make

Grammar
2 – 3 the 4 the 5 the 6 – 7 –
8 – 9 – 10 The 11 the 12 The
13 the 14 – 15 – 16 the

Reading
2 ~~for~~ as 3 ~~another~~ other
4 ~~what~~ which 5 ~~discuss~~ discussed
6 ~~off~~ up 7 ~~of~~ from 8 ✓
9 ~~Could~~ Would 10 ~~on~~ out
11 ~~informations~~ information

Writing
Sample answer
**Report on our company's use of the
Internet and social media**
Introduction
The purpose of this report is to summarise
how our company, Ekaterinburg Hats, uses
the Internet and social media and to make
recommendations for how we can use the
media more effectively.
Internet
At present, we use the Internet in quite
conventional ways. We transmit data using
email and we have a website in Russian
and English, where we show our products,
allow customers to contact us and post
company news. There is one member
of staff whose part-time duties include
updating the information and answering
queries, which come at about one a month.
However, most of our sales occur through
stores which stock our products. We
have few visits to our website, little direct
contact with end users of our products
and no means of selling directly to the
public. This means that our internet
presence is probably under-utilised.
Recommendations
I believe we could build a more dynamic
website by including web and social media
addresses on our packaging. This would
give customers a chance to contact us
directly, comment on our designs and give
us a useful extra market-research tool.

Unit 18

Vocabulary
1 2 way 3 ways 4 methods
2 2 C 3 B 4 D 5 C 6 B 7 C 8 A
   9 D 10 B

Grammar
1 2 the fact that 3 due to 4 owing
   5 why 6 result
2 *Suggested answers*
   2 will be able to work entirely
      from home because they will be
      connected online.
   3 to fall because lights and computers
      will become more efficient.
   4 to be full of people because most
      work will be done by machines.
   5 take management decisions because
      it will be able to assess different
      factors more efficiently than people.
   6 greener due to stricter government
      regulations.

Writing
Sample answer
**Proposal for reducing the negative effect
of our activities on the environment**
I have identified three areas of our working
methods which may be harmful to the
environment, and the purpose of this
proposal is to suggest ways in which we
can minimise any damage.
Firstly, each member of staff works with
their own personal computer, which, in
many cases, they do not turn off or put
on standby when they are not at their
desks. Secondly, office lights are left
on at night, apparently in the interests
of security. Thirdly, employees are in
the habit of printing out hard copies of
documents.
The first two things lead to much higher
power consumption than is necessary, with
its consequent effect on global warming.
The third means we use much more paper
than we should, which is wasteful of trees
and energy.
I suggest that we implement a policy of
hot-desking, where employees use any
computer which happens to be available,
and that it is made company policy to
turn off computers and office lights at the
end of the working day. Furthermore, all

printing out of computer documents should be prohibited unless strictly necessary. These measures would reduce damage to the environment while at the same time cutting down on company costs.

Unit 19

Vocabulary

1 2 staff turnover   3 long hours
4 work–life   5 motivated   6 off sick
7 productivity   8 bonus scheme
9 staff retention

2 2 A   3 C   4 B   5 A

Grammar

1 2 'I work for a bank in New York.'
3 'I have never worked in accounts before.'
4 'I have already printed out the sales forecast.'
5 'I'll fix the meeting for three o'clock tomorrow.'
6 'I can't speak (to you) because I'm busy.'
7 'We/They might/may change the computer system next year.'
8 'We/They bought new software last month.'
9 'The sales figures are bad.'

2 2 My boss ordered me to go to Berlin on the next plane.
3 I informed them that there had been a 3% drop in market share.
4 She requested Helga to phone the suppliers.
5 I enquired when she could deliver the goods.
6 I promised my boss that I'd have the/that report on his desk by midday the next/following day.
7 The project leader answered that they didn't know how much the development costs would be.

3 2 He told t̶o̶ me that the package had been sent the day before.
3 She explained **to** him / **told** him that she would prefer flexible working to part-time working.
4 He answered that he had changed jobs **last year / in the last year / the previous year / the year before**.

5 She asked him how much d̶i̶d̶ the flights cost.
6 He promised me that he **would** send the goods last week.
7 The caller enquired when **the product would** be launched.
8 He explained that he **had** forgotten to send the invoice.
9 He ordered her **to sign** the cheque for $10,000.
10 I told him **not to** send the application by email.

Unit 20

Vocabulary

1 g   2 d   3 c   4 a   5 h   6 f   7 e   8 b

Grammar

1 1 hadn't run; would not have made / wouldn't have made
2 had not decided / hadn't decided; would have been
3 would have achieved / 'd have achieved
4 would have been; had cut
5 had made; would have made / 'd have made

2 *Suggested answers*
2 would have chosen law.
3 the bank if I had known how hard the work is.
4 would have emigrated to Canada.
5 I had got such a good degree.

Reading

2 do   3 are   4 time   5 ✓   6 made
7 a   8 is   9 to   10 do   11 ✓   12 ✓
13 to   14 be   15 giving   16 month

Writing

Sample answer
Dear Mr Barraclough,
Thank you for your letter of 10 February in which you express interest in marketing your products in our country. I believe there is a very profitable potential market for your products, and we would definitely be interested in the possibility of acting as your agent here.
We would be delighted to meet you when you visit our country. May I suggest either 18 or 19 March?
Yours sincerely,

Unit 21

Vocabulary

2 C   3 A   4 C   5 D   6 A   7 A   8 D
9 D   10 B   11 A   12 D   13 D   14 C
15 B

Grammar

1   2 which/that/–   3 which/that/–
    4 what   5 whose   6 where   7 why
    8 What   9 who   10 whose

2   2   Did you repair the computer that/
        which wasn't working?
    3   I phoned the customer whose
        invoice hadn't arrived.
    4   We stayed at an excellent hotel
        (which was) near the city centre.
    5   I work for a software company
        whose headquarters are in Silicon
        Valley.
    6   Have you visited the factory where
        they make the components?
    7   Claudio is the technician who knows
        how to install the equipment.
    8   We'll hold the meeting at 11 o'clock
        when everyone is free.
    9   You forgot to answer the letter (that/
        which) I wrote.

Unit 22

Vocabulary

2 good   3 wide; huge
4 serious; tremendous   5 large

Grammar

2 with   3 about   4 with   5 of   6 for
7 to   8 with   9 of   10 with/against
11 on   12 in

Writing

1   2 resulted   3 led   4 caused
    5 result/consequence   6 due/owing

2   *Sample answer*
    Carmel Sun Creams: report on sales
    Our sales remained steady from January
    to February at €80,000.
    However, in March, they rose to
    €90,000 before falling to €60,000 in
    April as a result of the end of the skiing
    season.
    Our advertising campaign in April led to
    a rise in sales in May, which peaked in
    June at €140,000.
    Unfortunately, however, as a
    consequence of bad weather in June,
    sales fell temporarily to €80,000 in July.
    When the main holiday season started
    in August, it caused our sales to rise
    to €170,000, although these decreased
    to €60,000 in October as a result of the
    end of the summer holiday season.
    The start of the skiing season in
    November resulted in a rise in sales of
    €40,000 to reach €100,000 at the end of
    the year.

Unit 23

Vocabulary

1   2 last   3 last   4 latest
2   a   2 e   3 b/g   4 g/b   5 a/h   6 f
        7 c   8 h/a
    b   2   meet your requirements
        3   organise a face-to-face meeting
        4   do trouble-free business
        5   do/carry out construction work
        6   calculate costs
        7   extend our range of services
        8   organise work schedules
3   2 dissatisfied   3 delivery
    4 confidential   5 unreliable
    6 inefficient   7 extensive
    8 guaranteed   9 valued

Grammar

2   Unfortunately, Central Europe was hit
    by heavy storms last week and, as a
    consequence (of this), we have fallen
    behind with our deliveries.
3   There was a power cut in our area last
    week. This meant (that) our computer
    system was down.
4   Our suppliers were late sending us
    some components. As a result, we were
    unable to complete your order on time.
5   I am pleased to inform you that our
    suppliers have given us a considerable
    discount. Consequently, we are in a
    position to offer you the goods you
    have ordered at a reduced price.
6   Unfortunately, my secretary copied your
    telephone number incorrectly. This
    meant (that) I was unable to contact you.

Unit 24

Vocabulary

1   2 C   3 A   4 A   5 D   6 A   7 B
    8 D   9 A   10 A   11 C   12 B   13 D
    14 A   15 D

2 2 Firstly   3 because that way
4 To take a personal example
5 However   6 Secondly   7 You see
8 Finally
9 If you bear those things in mind

Grammar

1 2 having/encountering/finding
3 point   4 worth   5 no   6 It
2 *Suggested answers*
1 looking at online job advertisements.
2 staying in cheap hotels because it causes a bad impression.
3 doing all the talking – you've got to listen as well.
4 explaining exactly what I do.
5 buying things just because they're cheap – it's better to buy the things which do the job most efficiently.
6 getting promoted.

Writing supplement

Punctuation

1 2 f   3 g   4 b   5 h   6 a   7 c
  8 h   9 i   10 e

2 *Suggested answers*
  b Seville   c English   d Spanish
  e Mr Aziz   f Marketing Manager

3 To: Gonzalo Punzal
  Subject: Re: Visit to Seville
  Dear Mr Punzal,
  Unfortunately, I won't be able to meet
  you on the dates you mentioned as I
  already have a trip to Austria booked
  for that week. However, if you are
  free, the first week in May would be a
  very convenient time for me to come
  and see how the Spanish manufacture
  components.
  When I was last in Seville about
  three years ago, I stayed at the Hotel
  Inglaterra, which is right in the city
  centre. Would that be the best hotel
  to stay at on this occasion, or can you
  recommend somewhere else? Also,
  I hope to visit you with three or four
  colleagues if that is OK, because we
  hope to place quite a large order. As
  we will need to look at the figures quite
  closely, one of the team will be the Chief
  Accountant, Mr Felahi. The Operations
  Manager, the Production Manager and
  his assistant will also be coming.
  Please let me know if the suggested
  dates are convenient for you.
  Yours sincerely,
  Ahmed Aziz
  Chief Executive

4 2 team, who   3 However, we
  4 Hotel Alfonso XIII
  5 XIII, which   6 city, we
  7 stay. Therefore   8 Therefore, could
  9 you, your   10 accountant and
  11 Yours sincerely   12 sincerely,

Spelling

1 2 B   3 A   4 B   5 A   6 B   7 A
  8 A   9 B   10 B   11 A   12 B
  13 B   14 A   15 A   16 B   17 A
  18 A   19 B   20 A   21 B   22 B

2 ~~greatful~~ grateful
  ~~recomend~~ recommend
  ~~posible~~ possible
  ~~preferrence~~ preference
  ~~excelent~~ excellent
  ~~oportunity~~ opportunity
  ~~busineses~~ businesses
  ~~sugest~~ suggest
  ~~wich~~ which
  ~~begining~~ beginning
  ~~froward~~ forward

3 2 b   3 e   4 c   5 a   6 d   7 g

4 2 occurred   3 tried   4 phoning
  5 informed   6 speaking   7 mentioned
  8 running   9 crashing   10 developed
  11 coming   12 hoping   13 planning
  14 starting   15 referring   16 ironed

5 *Sample answer*
  Dear Ashram
  Melanie is in meetings all day, but she
  has asked me to reply on her behalf.
  As a result of the computers crashing,
  we had a very frustrating morning. Staff
  were unable to complete large amounts
  of routine work or answer emails. Also,
  they had to spend some time recovering
  work which had not been correctly
  saved when the system went down.
  All this could have been avoided if you
  had given us warning that this situation
  might occur. Could you please let us
  know in future when you are planning
  work of this sort so that we can take
  appropriate steps?
  Best wishes

Organising your writing
Paragraphing

1 a 3   b 2   c 6   d 5   e 1   f 4

2 *Suggested answers*
  paragraph 2: explaining the reason for
  writing (to get advice)
  paragraph 3: their requirements in some
  detail
  paragraph 4: rent (not buy)
  paragraph 5: inviting Lily to help further
  paragraph 6: rounding off

3 ... choice. // As I'm ...
  ... started. // I'd ...
  ... week. // One ...
  ... recruit. // I ...

4 See the email in Exercise 1 for a sample
  answer.

Linking paragraphs and ideas

1 a 1 When customers visit the site
    2 However 3 When they do this
    4 The advantage of this is that
    5 Unfortunately, though
    6 As a result

2 *Suggested answers*
paragraph 1: the reason for writing –
asking for help
paragraph 2: explaining one option
paragraph 3: explaining another option
paragraph 4: explaining the problem
with the second option
paragraph 5: repeating request

3 1 problems 2 customers 3 the option
of ordering and paying 4 registering
and saving credit-card details 5 the
website doesn't automatically bring up
their details 6 users 7 the problem
explained above 8 the problem
explained above

4 *Sample answer*
Hi Ricart,
We're having a bit of trouble with the
data projector in Meeting Room 2.
Basically, when it's been switched on
for some time during a presentation,
the screen starts to flicker. As a result
of this, people attending meetings in
that room find it hard on their eyes and
tend to stop watching the presentation.
Also, several managers are refusing to
use the room, which means that there is
overbooking for Meeting Room 1.
Could you please look at it? It may just
be a bad connection or perhaps the bulb
just needs changing. If you can't fix the
problem, the projector will need to be
changed.
Please give this priority, as we have
several presentations to clients in the
next few days.
Many thanks,

Planning letters and emails

1/2 Paragraph 1: d   Paragraph 2: c
Paragraph 3: f, b, a   Paragraph 4: e

3 b *Sample answer*
    Dear Sirs,
    We are a Marine Electronics
    company based in Genoa, Italy,
    specialising in navigation equipment
    for yachts.

At present we are looking for a
graphic design company to update
and redesign our product brochure
to give it a more modern, attractive
look. Our customers are mainly
weekend sailors throughout Europe
and North America. What we are
looking for is a brochure which
combines attractive photographs and
copy with technical specifications.
Your company is one of several that
have been recommended to us by
associates, and we would be grateful
if you could supply us with some
sample designs, accompanied by
some indication of how much the
work would cost. I am attaching our
current brochure as a pdf file for you
to work from.
If you need any more information,
please get in touch.
We look forward to hearing from
you.
Yours faithfully,

4 *Suggested answer*
The writer will want to achieve the
following: all errors made by QB
Supplies to be corrected; a change in
attitude by QB Supplies' employees;
better service in the future.

6 For sample answer, see page 66.

7 2 2 The main problem has been that
    3 For example
    4 with the result that
    5 In another instance
    6 In addition to these problems
    7 This has meant
    8 Finally
    9 I would like to remind you that

Linking ideas in short emails

1 *Suggested underlining:* In order to;
because; With this in mind

2 1 Could you please check that all fire
    exits are working properly?
  2 we will be holding a fire practice
  3 a to comply with local fire
       regulations
     b we want people to treat it as if it
       was a real emergency

3 1 In order to 2 this 3 this meant
  4 which

4 For sample answers, see pages 66–67.

5 1 1 order 2 which/that 3 as
   4 while/when
   2 Dear Mr Kreisky,
   I would be grateful if you could
   explain why we still have not received
   the eight computers which we
   purchased from your store last week.
   It is essential that you deliver them
   immediately, as we have just taken
   on new staff as part of our expansion
   and they need the computers in order
   to work efficiently.
   Yours sincerely,
   3 1 I'm happy to say
   2 in order to help
   3 While I'm there 4 with the aim of

Planning reports and proposals
2 For sample answer, see page 67
(completed version below).

3 *Sample answer*

Report on graduate recruitment at Bendex, SA

Introduction
The purpose of this report is to
summarise how we currently find
and take on graduate trainees and to
recommend changes to the system.

First contact
At present, we recruit graduates by
advertising vacancies through university
careers services. Students complete
an application form and need a
recommendation from a teacher or tutor.
We filter these applications and invite
suitable applicants to a preliminary
interview. Applicants who pass
this interview then do a series of
psychometric tests, along with further
more demanding interviews before
being selected.

Comments
The system works reasonably well.
About 45 applicants normally attend the
preliminary interview. From these, we
select 20 to go through the other parts
of the process. Our average graduate
intake is seven graduates a year, and
their quality has been very satisfactory.
However, each year two or three of
these recruits tend to leave the company
because they want more responsibility
than we initially offer.

Recommendations
I recommend that we give applicants
clearer information about what their
jobs will involve before they start.
I would also suggest that we try to
match the job possibilities more closely
to our candidates' aspirations, as many
of them are highly ambitious.

4 *Sample plan*
Paragraph 1: aim
Paragraph 2: next-door premises – not
necessary to expand there
Paragraph 3: city centre – too expensive
+ competition
Paragraph 4: near station – less
expensive + young people

5 For sample answer, see page 68.

6 **Proposal for expansion of Musicbug Stores in Mannheim**
The aim of this proposal is to suggest
an opportunity for expansion in
Mannheim.

At present, we have one store
located in the old city. We could
expand into the premises next to ours
without difficulty. However, I would
not recommend this, because we are
meeting demand from our customers
with no problems.

In order to extend our market,
I suggest that we should open new
premises in another district of the city.
I have found two possible locations.

The first is in the city centre, but
unfortunately the rent is rather high
at €12,000 a month. Also, two of our
competitors already have shops in the
area.

The second option is empty premises
opposite the main railway station.
I favour this, because many young
people go past this location every day.
What is more, it is less expensive than
the city centre.